Jeopardy!
and Philosophy

Popular Culture and Philosophy® Series Editor: George A. Reisch

For full details of all Popular Culture and Philosophy® books, visit www.opencourtbooks.com.

Popular Culture and Philosophy®

Jeopardy! and Philosophy

What Is Knowledge in the Form of a Question?

Edited by

SHAUN P. YOUNG

OPEN COURT
Chicago and LaSalle, Illinois

Volume 72 in the series, Popular Culture and Philosophy ®, edited by George A. Reisch

To order books from Open Court, call toll-free 1-800-815-2280, or visit our website at www.opencourtbooks.com.

Open Court Publishing Company is a division of Carus Publishing Company.

Printed and bound in the United States of America.

Library of Congress Cataloging-in-Publication Data

Jeopardy! and philosophy : what is knowledge in the form of a question? / edited by Shaun P. Young.
     p. cm. — (Popular culture and philosophy ; vol. 72)
    Includes bibliographical references and index.
    ISBN 978-0-8126-9799-5 (trade paper : alk. paper)
     1. Jeopardy! (Television program) 2. Games—Philosophy. I. Young, Shaun P.
    PN1992.77.J363J46 2012
    791.45'72—dc23

                                          2012032004

This book is dedicated to my mother, Eleanore Leet,
a long-time *Jeopardy!* fan, who, in the most fundamental
of senses (and many more), has made this possible.

Contents

A Champion's Philosophical Reflection

KEN JENNINGS

The syntactic conceit behind *Jeopardy!*'s "answer-in-the-form-of-a-question" gimmick is, of course, perfectly ridiculous.

If I were to ask someone, "What is Belgium?" I would be confused and possibly angry if the answer that came back was, "If you've lived the high life in this Low Country, you've probably dined on waterzooi, a classic dish." Wait, what? Surely that's not the definition of Belgium. "Well, Fabiola de Mora y Aragon of Spain was a December bride; she married Baudouin, king of this country in 1960." *How is that an answer, Trebek?* I might roar, shaking my cryptic tormentor by his slim, sinewy Canadian shoulders.

When people in North America ask me about *Jeopardy!*, they have many questions: how long I was on the show (a few months), is it rigged (no), what the host is like (very nice and funny), and many others. But people outside North America almost always say the same thing: "Is that the quiz show with the questions and answers reversed? Why do they do that? It doesn't make any sense."

In North America, we've been used to the oddity for almost fifty years. We don't even notice it anymore. In fact, quiz nerds here often inadvertently borrow the "What is . . . ?" phrasing when they play in non-*Jeopardy!* events like quiz bowl or pub trivia, to the merriment of all. The host may rib them a bit, but no one's really surprised.

But the form-of-a-question silliness is, I think, a central part of the show's success. If the only acceptable "What is Belgium?" answer were "A constitutional monarchy between

France and the Netherlands, capital Brussels," the way it is in real life, what a dreary TV show that would be. Instead, *Jeopardy!* exists in a parallel universe of endlessly surprising factual connections and digressions.

What is Belgium? Well, this country's King Leopold III spent much of World War II as a prisoner in his own castle. Lambic beer, fermented by wild yeasts, is mainly made here. In 2011, this nation with two distinct ethnic groups broke a record by marking 249 days without a government. On planet *Jeopardy!*, every topic is *big*, revealing more and more detail, like a beautiful fractal, the closer you look. Even Belgium contains multitudes.

To many of the show's most dedicated fans, myself included, that's precisely the appeal. The world is full of a wealth of information, and no TV series pelts it at your head and upper torso faster than *Jeopardy!* does. There are no long, dramatic, *Millionaire*-style pauses and orchestra hits here. The point seems to be to dazzle the audience as brightly as possible with the miraculous complexity of the universe, sixty-one questions per half hour, on every conceivable topic from Children's Literature to Particle Physics to Jazz.

Even better, the show requires its contestants to actually *know* these facts in mere seconds, off the tops of their heads. You don't have a few minutes to phone a friend or ask the audience, consult Google or your smartphone. We live in an age where facts are so easily accessible that it often seems pointless to bother *learning* things, but *Jeopardy!* is stubbornly old-school; it still rewards you for being curious enough to internalize those facts, take them in and make them part of yourself. Real-life decisions, of course, require a foundation of thousands of correct facts as well, and so residents of planet *Jeopardy!* become better residents of planet Earth as well: more informed citizens, more reliable analysts, more unexpected connectors of ideas, more interesting conversationalists.

Beyond questions about *Jeopardy!* being rigged or what Alex Trebek is like, I'm sometimes asked a question that's a little more existentially disturbing: how did you know all that stuff? I'm not a professional philosopher like the contributors to this volume; I don't have to wave my finger and reply, airily, "Ah, how do any of us really 'know' anything?" But I do feel like I am implicitly being asked for The Secret, some memory technique or dietary supplement that can make a *Jeopardy!* champion out of anyone.

The truth, I'm afraid, is much more humdrum. *Jeopardy!* champions are congenitally curious. We are sponges for information—and not just about our pet interests, like everyone tends to remember, but about any subject at all. We are omnivorous, and we crave knowledge for its own pleasurable sake, not because we think we know what we're going to do with it later. One *Jeopardy!* champ called the ideal preparation for the show "a lifetime of paying attention," and I think that's exactly right.

In other words, anyone can be *Jeopardy!* material. It has nothing to do with answering in the form of a question—it's about *living your life* in the form of a question, constantly on the lookout for novelty, inquisitive about everything that happens to you. If there truly is a philosophy of *Jeopardy!*, I suppose that's it in a nutshell: that knowing stuff matters, that the facts in your head matter. In fact, what we call the Self is probably, in large part, the accumulation of those facts.

On planet Earth, not every contest is won by the most knowledgeable side, but thank goodness there's always planet *Jeopardy!* The customs there may be different. Time seems to pass more quickly. The dominant life-forms are a little odd—they wear more sweaters and talk about their cats more than we do—but usually we can see ourselves in them, aspire to their easy mastery. I only got to live on planet *Jeopardy!* for a few months, and I still miss it. Some nights I dream about it. At least, like millions of others, I still get to visit for half an hour every weeknight.

Check local listings.

Acknowledgments

Every book represents the collective efforts of a number of people—something that is especially true with regard to edited collections. I would like to thank the contributors for their very interesting and enjoyable chapters, without which this book, literally, would not exist. I would also like to extend my immense appreciation to George Reisch and David Ramsay Steele, not only for the opportunity to serve as editor for this wonderful volume, but also for their endless patience, guidance, and support. Though it may not always be self-evident, their contribution has been enormous and critical. I would also like to give special thanks to Robert Arp, who, along with George, David, and myself, helped to write the Answers and Questions found at the end of each section of the book. I am very grateful to Ken Jennings for his wonderful reflection on the character and appeal of *Jeopardy!* Finally, and as always, I want to thank my wife, Kate Bird, and our daughters Amy and Faith, for their love, support, and patience.

A Quiz Show, Some Fans, and a Lot of Fun: What Is *Jeopardy! and Philosophy?*

SHAUN P. YOUNG

On March 30th, 1964, television viewers were treated to a new quiz show that turned the traditional format of quiz shows on its head. In this new show, the host read answers for which contestants were required to provide the questions—what's been labeled the "answer-and-question" format. According to the show's creator, television impresario and entertainment mogul Merv Griffin, this unconventional approach was suggested by his wife, Julann.[1] As they say, the rest is history!

Jeopardy! is "America's Favorite Quiz Show®," averaging nine million viewers daily. Royalty, presidents, movie stars, television personalities, famous athletes, and a host of Nobel laureates have presented clues or been contestants on the show. Since 1984, it has outlived three hundred competitors, received twenty-nine Daytime Emmy Awards, and both *TV Guide* and the *Game Show Network* (GSN) ranked *Jeopardy!* #2 among the Fifty Greatest Game Shows of All Time.[2]

Jeopardy! has achieved an iconic status within popular culture, regularly serving as a source of reference and parody on popular television and in movies, novels and music. Some of the most popular television shows of all time, including *The Simpsons*, *Saturday Night Live*, *Cheers*, and *The Golden Girls*, to name but a few, have used *Jeopardy!* with hilarious effect. "Weird Al" Yankovic did likewise with his song "I Lost on

---

[1] Cynthia Lowry, "Merv Griffin: Question and Answer Man," Associated Press, *Independent Star-News* (March 29th, 1964).

[2] See "Jeopardy!" Wikipedia, <http://en.wikipedia.org/wiki/Jeopardy!>.

Jeopardy." More seriously, *Jeopardy!* has also been used as an instructional tool by a variety of national educators. And the participation of "Watson"—the IBM-developed supercomputer—brought to widespread public attention the development of "artificial intelligence" and added a new and exciting element to the show: the long-imagined competition between humans and machines.

The show has evolved with the passage of time. Contestants on the show range in age from ten upwards, and its reach now extends to electronic gaming systems, Facebook, and the Twitterverse. Each month its official website (www.jeopardy.com) receives upwards of four hundred thousand visits. The most successful *Jeopardy!* contestants—Ken Jennings, Brad Rutter, Frank Spangenberg, for example—have appeared on late-night talk shows, received book contracts, and been interviewed by major newspapers, treatment that is substantially different than, say, the treatment received by the winners of *The Price Is Right*, *Who Wants to Be a Millionaire?* or *Deal or No Deal*. Ken Jennings and Brad Rutter have both become millionaires as a result of the show!

What explains the show's overwhelming and continuing success? There are numerous possible answers to that question, among which must certainly be the diversity of topics from which questions are drawn. Contestants are asked to answer questions concerning everything from "Geometry" to "Central American Wildlife" to "Car Pets" and "Historical Twits," and almost everything in between. When that fact is coupled with the establishment of separate categories for kids, teens, college students, and champions, *Jeopardy!* provides a forum in which almost all who wish to can participate in friendly competition, whether in the studio as official contestants or in the comfort of their home (where we can be secure in the knowledge that we could surpass Ken Jennings's record, if only we had the time to participate in person!).

Those features of *Jeopardy!* generate a veritable cornucopia of topics that are ripe for philosophical exploration. This book looks at questions such as: Is *Jeopardy!* a "good" game? Does it educate or merely entertain? Does it celebrate particular values, principles or beliefs? What can it teach us about artificial intelligence and the social benefits of a liberal education? And, perhaps most importantly, would Ken Jennings survive on *Survivor*?

Those questions are answered through an examination of various aspects of the show, including its revolutionary format and its unparalleled success both as a television show and a recognized icon of popular culture. Contributors include professional philosophers, other academics, and writers—a couple of whom are, themselves, *Jeopardy!* champions (though, thankfully, they have managed to avoid the restricting degree of celebrity suffered by Ken Jennings). There are also 'answers' for readers to ponder, so that they might get their fix of *Jeopardy!* without having to put down the book.

I'm willing to wager that this book will delight and stimulate all those armchair *Jeopardy!* champions among us.

I'll Take Popular Culture, Alex

Here are the Answers
(For the Questions, see page 187)

1. This Canadian is the face of America's favorite TV game show.

2. This long-lived scifi hero made his TV debut the day after John Kennedy was killed.

3. This rock group celebrated its fiftieth anniversary in 2012.

4. Conceived by Robert Kirkman, this post-apocalyptic comic book series was made into a TV drama serial commencing in 2010.

5. He has won the most money of any *Jeopardy!* contestant.

6. This is the best selling book in Open Court's Popular Culture and Philosophy series.

7. The first episode of this popular TV drama series begins with the arrival of news of the sinking of the *Titanic*.

8. He created *Buffy the Vampire Slayer*, *Firefly*, and *Dollhouse*.

9. In this TV show, Shawn Spencer pretends his natural abilities are supernatural.

10. Her real name is Stefani Joanne Angelina Germanotta.

11. This critic of popular culture first made his name with a book about heavy metal bands in North Dakota.

12. When Snoop Dogg changed his name to Snoop Lion following a religious experience, he disclosed that he was the reincarnation of this earlier performer.

13. Based on a 2004 novel by Jeff Lindsay, this TV show centers on a like-able repeat offender.

14. The 2002 movie *I Am Trying to Break Your Heart* is about this Chicago-based alternative rock band.

15. Despite the latitude, there's plenty of ice in Albuquerque, according to this explosive TV drama.

16. This 1957 quiz show champion cheated by getting both the questions and the answers in advance.

17. This British movie actor played Charles Van Doren in the 1994 movie *Quiz Show*.

18. This band was wound up following the sudden death of its drummer in 1980.

19. This 2001 fantasy novel featured one-eyed Mr. Wednesday.

20. Lorenzo von Matterhorn is the fake identity of a philanderer in this TV comedy series.

21. Contrary to what many fans suppose, this man in black never did time.

22. This political movement, begun in late 2008 or early 2009, is named for an event in December 1773.

23. This was the first volume to appear in Open Court's Popular Culture and Philosophy series.

24. More of his stories have been made into movies than those of any other author.

25. This 1964 movie about a rock group was made hastily on a low budget because its backers didn't believe the group's popularity could last.

26. This 1951 tale of a maladjusted teenager has never been made into a movie.

27. He created the TV shows *Seinfeld* and *Curb Your Enthusiasm*.

28. 221B Baker Street.

29. He wrote the stories that became *Blade Runner*, *Minority Report*, and *Total Recall*.

30. This familiar book is Volume 72 in Open Court's Popular Culture and Philosophy series.

I

America's
Favorite
Quiz Show

1

Jeopardy! and American Exceptionalism

DANIEL F. MELIA

I have achieved the American Dream; I have won a car on television. This overstatement about success is mildly amusing because it's true; perhaps also a little eccentric in my case since people expect "Berkeley Professors" to be unconcerned with such mundane and material expressions of personality as their cars, particularly if acquired by competing on a literally "trivial" television quiz show.

Besides, I chose a Corvette, an overpowered, adolescent dream car if ever there was one. However even Berkeley professors more august and austere than I set some store by the ethos projected by their cars. The Dwinelle Hall parking lot at UC Berkeley these days looks like a Prius dealer's showroom—which makes a change since it used to look like a corporate display of Volvo station wagons.

A *Booklist* review of a car photo book, *Roadside America: The Automobile and the American Dream*, by Lucinda Lewis, puts it baldly: "One of pop culture's universal truths is that Americans have carried on an unabashed romance with the automobile since its invention around the turn of the twentieth century." Aldous Huxley was not far off in 1932 when he had his characters in *Brave New World* making the sign of the "T" in memorial worship of Henry Ford and his first great automotive creation. It's difficult to imagine contestants on British or German game shows jumping up and down and yelling at the very mention of the fact that they *might* win a car, but a glance at YouTube is all it takes to see that it is normal behavior on American game shows.

America's fascination with the automobile does not require deep analysis to link to a larger set of cultural attitudes and values. America is big. The traditional way to make your way or to escape annoying entanglements or to reinvent yourself is, as Huckleberry Finn puts it, to "light out for the territory." As Horace Greeley famously said, "Go West, young man" (although at the time he was talking about Illinois!).

Driving a car is an American rite of passage, symbolizing our adherence to the values of personal autonomy and freedom to travel at a moment's notice. De Tocqueville never saw an automobile, but he would have recognized its appeal to his new Americans. *Jeopardy!* no longer awards cars to five-game winners (and, in fact, no longer restricts winning to five regular-season games) but in every other respect is a kind of model not only of American television game shows, but of a particular set of American values which, in their profile, differ from those of other cultures.

One way of defining a "culture" is as a set of values shared by some group of people that does not overlap perfectly with the values of another set of people. What constitutes living the good life, a question that has interested philosophers since ancient Athens, for a great many modern Americans apparently involves having a really cool car. Winning one in public, on television, apparently enhances the experience of "good living."

I'll Take American Values for $2,000, Alex

Jeopardy! was begotten in the wake of the Quiz Show Scandals of the 1960s. In 1964, casting about for an idea for a new game show, and one which could evade the accusation of giving the contestants the answers, Merv Griffin asked his wife for her ideas. She replied (according to Merv's story) "5,280 feet." "What is a mile?" replied Merv, and the problem was solved.

The gimmick of the show was that the contestants were given the *answers* ON THE AIR, IN PUBLIC, and had to come up with the *questions*. Notably, contestants had to frame their responses in the form of a question. ("Who is George Washington, Alex?") Additionally, wrong answers carried the penalty of a loss of the money value of the clue, hence the show's name. The answer-in-the-form-of-a-question format is merely a semantic evasion, but the public was apparently ready for a new quiz show, and *Jeopardy!* has been on the air in two incarnations since 1964. *Jeopardy!*'s extraordinary longevity (1964–79 and 1984 to at least 2014 under the current contract) underlines and validates its status as a mirror of general American cultural values. *Jeopardy!*'s central characteristics give at least a partial answer to the question, "What does it mean to be an American, Alex?"

People like what they value. Fads (*Jersey Shore* and its clones, *American Idol* and its ilk) come and go. "Entertainment" that lasts for decades clearly speaks to the culture it addresses. So how does *Jeopardy!* exemplify a specifically American set of values, of things that Americans think define them and their culture, things that constitute "living well" as an American?

And Here Are Today's Categories . . .
Individual Agonistic Display

It's not that other cultures don't enjoy contests; it's just that we seem to require them in a great many more venues. Compare the huge success in the US of *Survivor*, which pits poorly prepared people against one another for thirty-nine days in a remote wilderness, with its very weak performance in Europe. Much more popular in the UK was *I'm a Celebrity, Get Me Out of Here*, which used a similar format to expose the weaknesses of minor celebrities under similar circumstances; the contest being secondary to the ridicule.

In *Big Brother*, a dozen or so people are confined in closed house and garden for a month with no outside contact (or reading material) voting each other out one by one as the show progresses. European versions of the show are about humiliation (dividing the contestants into guards and prisoners, for instance) and class conflict ("You've never had to work a day in your life, you posh twit!" "You've never *wanted* to work a day in your life you dole-sucking parasite!") The American version, however, while it started by imitating the original Dutch version closely, has now evolved into a series of contests for Head of Household, and Veto Power, with the recriminations and class warfare severely limited, in terms of air-time at least.

Jeopardy! is pure contest: who gets on the show in the first place (about four hundred contestants per year out of twenty-four thousand or more people who take the qualifying test), who presses the signaling device first, who answers the questions correctly, and who places optimal bets on the Daily Doubles and Final Jeopardy!, all the while risking loss of their accumulated winnings by answering wrong. The same is true of the other two longest running game shows, *The Price Is Right*, and *Wheel of Fortune*. In each case you must compete against other contestants as well as against the show itself.

Why do Americans like this kind of competition? I think that the display of such "fair" competitions reinforces the American faith in classless meritocracy. We like to see an open contest with equal rules for all. We see no shame in losing such a contest to a better player on the day. *Jeopardy!,* by the way, like a political campaign, is winner take all. There is no advantage to saving, say five thousand dollars, at the end of the game. If you do not win, you get either two thousand dollars for second place or one thousand dollars for finishing third—probably just enough to cover your travel expenses to Los Angeles, which are not paid by the show, except during the annual tournament.

When *Jeopardy!* first appeared on television in 1964, contestants were permitted to ring in as soon as they thought that they knew the answers. This practice led to a faster-paced game and many more wrong guesses, but it was soon dropped in favor of the present system of allowing host Alex Trebek to complete the reading of the clue before making the contestant's signaling devices "live." The change was apparently made to allow the television audience to play along on an equal footing with the on-air players, thus emphasizing the equalitarian nature of the game.

The Price Is Right and *Wheel of Fortune* share this play-along structure. I have occasionally been clever enough to guess the correct solution on *Wheel of Fortune* while watching the show on television before Vanna White has turned over any of the letters! It's almost as good as being on the show, except you don't win any money.

Let's Make It a True Daily Double!
Redemption

In common with *The Price Is Right* and *Wheel of Fortune,* *Jeopardy!* has significant elements of possible redemption. First, there are the Daily Doubles, (one in the first round of the game, and two in the second round, in which the value of the clues is double that of the first round.) Daily Doubles allow the player who buzzes in on them to bet an amount up to the total of his winnings to that point in the game, or, up to the amount of the highest value clue in the round—one thousand dollars in round one, two thousand in round two.

The Daily Doubles are randomly placed on the board. So a contestant with only half the money of the leader can, at one stroke, share the lead. Likewise, the final question of the show, Final Jeopardy!, allows the players to bet all their accumulated money, also allowing for, and often producing, a come-from-behind victory. *Wheel of Fortune* has "bankrupt" and "lose a turn" spaces on the wheel that can derail a winning player's chance at a winning round, as well as a final round in which each player plays one turn at a time, also allowing for surprise comebacks.

In *The Price Is Right*, even contestants who have failed in their on-stage efforts to win prizes are given a chance to play in the big final round by spinning a wheel of fortune at two points in the game. *Survivor* and *Big Brother* have both brought ousted players back into the game, and *Survivor* actually created last season what they called "Redemption Island," where ousted players competed to get back in the main game (a ploy also adopted on *Top Chef Texas* this season.)

Winning the "Veto" contest in *Big Brother* allows the contestant to remove him or herself (or an ally) from consideration for eviction. *Survivor* contestants can win (or find) "immunity idols" that can be used to save them from eviction at the last minute. European game shows rarely if ever have these redemptive features. American society is permeated, to a degree scarcely imaginable outside it, with the Christian presumption of Redemption.

Game shows don't openly (or even, I suspect, covertly) rely on Jesus for redemption. They instead rely on the American adherence to notions of self-reinvention and second chances for everyone. This belief is of a piece with "lighting out for the territory." We can always start over, try something new, be a better person. Cassius Clay can become Muhammad Ali. Debutant Patty Hearst can become the revolutionary Tanya, and then suburban housewife Patty Hearst again. Marion Barry can be re-elected mayor of Washington DC in spite of the videotapes of him buying and using cocaine. General Motors can emerge from bankruptcy leaner, better, and more profitable. We can all diet, work out, study yoga, or tai chi, or vegan cooking, or whatever.

It's Not a "Buzzer", It's a "Signaling Device"!
Physical Tests

Jeopardy! has the dreaded buzzer, though if you call it that, someone on the show immediately corrects you to "signaling device." No one knows why. Maybe "buzzer" is trademarked. The *Jeopardy!* folks are dead serious about this, though.

The difficulty of the buzzer is easy to underestimate from a distance. It's a small tube, not unlike a thick ballpoint pen, with a button at the end to depress to "buzz in." The button has about a quarter of an inch of play before it makes contact. The trick is this: you are not allowed to buzz in until Alex Trebek has officially finished reading the "answer" prompt. When his mouth has closed at the end of the question for some small fragment of time, one of the *Jeopardy!* staff, at the writer's and producer's table out of the sight of the contestants, flicks a switch to activate the buzzers as well as a string of tiny lights, "go lights," (never shown on your home TV) around the Answer Board TV array.

If you buzz in before the switch is thrown your buzzer is locked out for one fifth of a second. If you tie with another buzzer, both buzzers are locked out for a fifth of a second. Here's the problem: if you wait until your brain has actually registered that the little lights have come on, you will almost certainly be too late. It's all about feeling the rhythm. In his excellent book about his triumphs and failures on *Jeopardy!* and in life, *Prisoner of Trebekistan*, Bob Harris explains the difficulty.

In the U.S., standard video zips by at 29.97 frames per second. In advanced games multiple players often twitch [the sign that they are buzzing in, even if the buzzer hand is out of sight] within three frames. So in tournament play all three thumbs might go *clicketyclicketyclick* in under one tenth of a second. Just for comparison, a 90-mph fast ball takes 0.45 seconds to reach the batter. Most coaches think it takes about half that time to recognize a pitch and begin a good swing. Therefore the reflex of a .300 hitter takes two tenths of a second. Twice as long. On rare occasions all three contestants will twitch within a single video frame. One third of one tenth of a second. About 30 milliseconds. (p. 180)

In tournament play, the little "go lights" are often not seen to go on by the contestants or the audience, as tungsten filaments take longer than that to begin to glow. *Wheel of Fortune* involves the contestants in bending over a bar and physically spinning a large horizontal wheel. *The Price Is Right* often has contestants rolling giant dice, dropping giant plinko chips, putting a golf ball, running back and forth to replace prices and pull levers and the like, not to mention spinning the giant, vertical "redemption" wheel. *Survivor* and *Big Brother* have extremely physical contests and races that have, on both shows, sometimes resulted in physical injury to the players.

Only rare European game shows have physical contests beyond pressing a buzzer. Really physical games like *It's a Knockout* are rarities, not the rule. Part of Americans' readiness for the frontier is, apparently, a psychological readiness to defeat the wilderness with our bare hands. When we have lit out for the territory, we evidently expect to build a sod house with our own hands and rassle bears whenever necessary.

What Is Preparation H.L. Mencken?
Improvisation

Because of the nature of many of the questions on *Jeopardy!* thinking creatively and improvisationally is a necessity for playing at all well. In addition to purely informational answers (called "pure trivia" by quiznerds) such as "Latin for 'swaddling clothes,' they're books printed before 1501, in the infancy of typography," (What are incunabula?) many *Jeopardy!* prompts require "teasing out" (quiznerds term again) the correct response. For example, in the Before and After category, "Sultan of Swat makes it to the Supreme Court" (who is Babe Ruth Bader Ginsburg?)

Confidence in your own ability to reason swiftly is essential to competing successfully at *Jeopardy!* because often you have to decide to buzz in before you actually call the answer to your mind. You have to judge "I know this" or "I don't know this" without actually coming up with the answer in your head, because if you wait until you are sure, the other contestants (and note the agonistic term) will eat your lunch.

In analyzing my own games, I have also noticed that a wrong answer rate of around ten percent is about right. Lower, and you are not buzzing in on enough questions to win, higher, and you will lose too much money to win. *The Price Is Right* requires contestants to estimate prices as closely as possible *without going over* the actual retail price and also presents contestants with a bewildering array of stupid activities as part of the guessing process. To win you need to be awfully lucky or pretty quick on your feet mentally.

In *Wheel of Fortune* (essentially the one letter at a time spelling game known as *Ghost*) you need to be able to recognize word and phrase shapes faster than the other players in order to win. *Big Brother* and *Survivor* both depend upon constantly changing strategy to keep your allies and evict your enemies as the numbers of both dwindle and the need to betray your allies grows. On the American frontier, you apparently still need to be ready for anything: Indians, strange animals, alkali water and Jimson weed; gold.

I Don't Usually Watch Television, But . . .
Middlebrow Sets of Knowledge

Among the most frequent categories on *Jeopardy!* over the years are: Literature, Science, World Geography, Shakespeare, Word Origins, US Presidents, State Capitals, American History, Opera, Ballet, Sports, and Business and Industry. It's common knowledge among *Jeopardy!* geeks that all Belgian surrealists are René Magritte, all Finnish composers are Sibelius, and all American silversmiths are Paul Revere. What has often been derided as "middlebrow" culture, as opposed to the superior "highbrow" variety, is actually a set of cultural commonplaces, things generally regarded as worth reading, knowing, seeing, tasting, and visiting even by those with little or no interest in the particular cultural items that make up the set.

The person who has seen a summer stock production or film version of Shakespeare's *Julius Caesar* is a middlebrow. The person who knows that Shakespeare's source for the story was Plutarch's *Lives* and who has seen it performed by the Royal Shakespeare Company used to be called a highbrow, but in our present postmodern world of cultural fragmentation is probably called a drama nerd.

The virtue of middlebrow culture, formerly exemplified by such events as the *Ed Sullivan Show*, the Boston Pops, *Life* magazine, and the Book of the Month Club, is that it defines things that are thought by many to be worth something both to individual "culture" and to the cultural life of the community. These are things with ascribed value in the culture and, as such, represent what the culture considers "good" and worth incorporating in your life. If you wish to live the (American) good life, these are things you must know, if only to reject some of them. Middlebrow taste is a powerful form of communication within a society and between societies. Americans have bought a lot of tickets to the films of Jerry Lewis; the French have made him a Commander of the Legion of Honor.

The concentration of categories on *Jeopardy!* and the repetitive information required to respond to the questions correctly is a kind of primer of middlebrow cultural information. *Jeopardy!* players are expected to know the name and reputation of Magritte as a Belgian surrealist, but not that of his colleague and collaborator E.L.T. Mesens. Accepted canons of knowledge have fragmented everywhere, but *Jeopardy!* keeps both the notion and the substance of this sort of valuable, communicative, cultural capital alive in its American incarnation. Bob Harris wrote, flatteringly, that he was initially worried about facing me in the *Jeopardy!* tournament because he judged that I had actually read all the books that he had memorized the titles of, thus nicely drawing the brow line between middle- and high-.

Unsurprisingly, many who consider themselves intellectuals have mixed or negative feelings about television, let alone about television game shows. Winning prizes and money can potentially be seen as too detached from actual work to be morally admirable, and certainly many in a university environment consider themselves to be deep and complex thinkers, above the recall of mere "trivia." Hugh of St. Victor, the twelfth-century thinker, urged, "Learn everything, and you will see afterward that nothing is useless," but there seem to be many who believe that learning some sorts of things is indeed useless, or at least, wish to give the impression that some things are beneath them, the "highbrow wannabes." Even among

American intellectuals, it seems, there is an ironic thread of anti-intellectualism. "So, you think you're smarter than me?" remains the dark underbelly of American equalitarianism.

The fact that *Jeopardy!* attracts the kind of criticism it does is further evidence that it has a strong cultural presence. After my first appearance on *Jeopardy!* I was struck by how many of my university colleagues felt the need to explain to me that they had seen me on the show when they had picked up the baby-sitter, or driven past a hardware store with a TV in the window, or stopped next door to borrow a copy of Kierkegaard's *Fear and Trembling*. The only man amongst my professorial colleagues that Diogenes would have sought out was the late distinguished philosopher Wallace Matson who emailed me that I had "fulfilled his Walter Mitty fantasy." From my own point of view, rapid recall doesn't prove that you're smart, but neither does slow recall.

Final Jeopardy!

Part of Americans' view of ourselves is the sense that we're somehow different from other countries and peoples, even from those who are our own immediate ancestors. From the days of John Winthrop we have claimed that we are exceptional, even if many of us do not still have a literal belief that God has chosen us for special favor as a people.

While the days of nineteenth-century discussions of "national character" have gone the way of eugenics (and for much the same reason) it is possible to talk about differences between cultures, with "culture" taken to signify incompletely overlapping bell curves of behavior and belief in different populations, marked by language, geography, self-identification and the like.

We've all experienced the reality of this state of affairs, even in the face of increasing globalization, when traveling to a new cultural environment. Compared to many other people on this earth, Americans talk too loudly, take up too much space even when just walking down the street, prefer quantity to quality in food, and tend to try to settle too many problems by the application of money. Not every American, not all the time, but a lot of us and a lot of the time. The French hold their elbows strangely close to their bodies; Italians wave their arms around. There are films of former Mayor Fiorello LaGuardia of New York in which it is possible to tell whether he is speaking English, Italian, or Yiddish solely by the way he uses his arms and hands.

Perhaps because we have continued to be a nation of immigrants, the US has a low-context, information-sharing culture, quite different from that of England or Japan, two nations whose customs and attitudes often puzzle American travelers. We are not offended if a newspaper editorial compares someone to "George Washington, the first President of the United States," while English newspapers do not explain to their readers who Winston Churchill or Charles the First were, because English people ought to know such things and are insulted to be talked to as if they did not know. Americans assume that some people may not know, and take no offense. Americans ask for information, and other Americans freely give them that information, without asking "Why do you want to know?"

Shows such as *Jeopardy! Wheel of Fortune,* and *The Price Is Right* spread information freely and reward those who have information and share it by playing the game well. They are low-context and information-sharing. These long-running game shows, and particularly *Jeopardy!,* are representative of several of the beliefs and attitudes that are central to Americans' understanding of their own character. They are indicators of many of the things that for Americans constitute living the best life. They constitute an index of cultural beliefs and activities which identify some of the deep differences between American culture and that of even our nearest cultural neighbors in Europe—the ways that we are, in fact, exceptional.

2

Are All *Jeopardy!* Contestants Created Equal?

SHAUN P. YOUNG

*E*quality is an idea that has acquired a great deal of significance, not only in philosophical circles, but in almost every area of life and all around the globe. Equality is an idea that has inspired philosophers, artists, activists, politicians, and military leaders, and has propelled revolutions.

The notion that all humans are equal, at least in certain important respects, began to gather support in the seventeenth century, featuring prominently in such works as Thomas Hobbes's *Leviathan* (1651) and John Locke's *Two Treatises of Government* (1689). In the eighteenth century it served as a foundational element of the US Declaration of Independence (1776)—the second paragraph of which begins with the statement: "We hold these truths to be self-evident, that all men are created equal, . . ."—and a rallying cry of the French Revolution (*Liberté, égalité, fraternité*).

Support for the idea has continued to grow, and equality is now generally understood to be an essential element of justice, whether we're talking about legal justice, political justice, social justice, or any other type of justice imaginable. Today, inequalities are typically condemned as injustices.

At first glance, *Jeopardy!* appears to embrace the idea of equality in a number of important ways. For example, all applicants and contestants are subject to the same demands and challenges: each must successfully complete a predetermined application process prior to being offered an initial opportunity to be a contestant on the show, and all contestants must abide by the same rules when playing the game. But does the appearance of equality survive a closer examination? If we look "behind the scenes" and "beneath the surface" does *Jeopardy!* satisfy the demands of equality?

Let's Meet Tonight's Contestants

Like "justice" and "liberty", "equality" is what philosopher Walter Gallie (1912–1998) labeled an "essentially contested concept"—a concept that's widely accepted but also the focus of significant disagreement regarding how it is best realized. A cursory review of past or current discussions concerning "equality" makes its essentially contested character readily apparent.

Since the time of Plato (429–347 B.C.E.), many famous and influential philosophers have devoted substantial effort to critically examining and developing the idea of equality. The result has been a number of different understandings of the requirements of equality. Aristotle (384–322 B.C.E.) argued that equality requires that equals be treated equally: we must "treat like cases as like." That means that, in certain circumstances, those possessing more intelligence or more skill than others, can legitimately be treated differently without violating the requirements of equality. In particular, when distributing the benefits associated with citizenship—such as the right to hold public office, to attend the governing assembly or to sit on juries—citizens can be treated "unequally" insofar as individuals who possess certain qualities can properly receive a greater share of the benefits relative to their fellow citizens. By "treating like cases as like," we achieve what Aristotle labels *proportional* equality and, by extension, justice. (Such an understanding is likely considered acceptable by only a small minority of people in contemporary western liberal democracies.)

Aristotelian proportional equality connects the idea of equality with that of *desert*: people should receive only what they deserve—nothing more, nothing less. By treating like cases as like, all are being treated in the manner they deserve. So, if the winning contestant on *Jeopardy!* receives $30,000 while the other two receive only parting gifts worth very little, it can be argued that the resulting inequality in compensation is justified because the winner played the game more effectively (that is, with greater skill) than his or her competitors, and therefore, given the rules of the game, the outcome is deserved.

It could be suggested that *Jeopardy!* employs an element of Aristotelian proportional equality insofar as there are different categories of contestants who compete only with their peers: kids, teens, college students, or champions. However, given the nature of the competition—knowledge is critical to success—and, consequently, the advantages that are usually associated with age and experience, it seems unlikely that many would consider it either unacceptable or illegitimate to segregate contestants in such a manner. Indeed, such segregation seems necessary in order to ensure as equal a "playing field" as is possible. For many the inequality generated by not doing so would be painful to watch and considered a source of legitimate criticism.

One reason for that sentiment is the fact that equality is generally now understood to be inextricably connected to human dignity: the realization of human dignity demands that all individuals be treated with equal concern and respect; only by so doing is it possible to respect every individual's humanity adequately—in other words, being human is a sufficient condition for deserving equal treatment. (Peter Singer has argued that such a perspective should be extended to nonhumans who possess the potential to experience pain and suffering, but I won't pursue that here, as we're not about to see any non-humans on *Jeopardy!*)

But what precisely is demanded by equality? Does it require that all individuals be provided identical resources (such as personal knowledge)? Or is it enough to ensure that all individuals have an equal opportunity to pursue their goals? And is enshrining any such requirement in regulations (such as government legislation or the rules that guide *Jeopardy!* contestants' behavior) adequate to ensure their realization?

And the Categories Are . . .

People who talk about equality, whether they praise it or disparage it, often disagree about what equality means. For some, equality properly concerns *outcomes*: individuals are treated equally when a given process or situation produces the same outcome for all. At the extreme, such a position supports the belief that all individuals should be provided an identical supply of goods and services.

However, few philosophers have supported such a stance. Perhaps it's more attractive or palatable if we narrow its application. For example, by providing all individuals who are successful at the application stage with an assured chance to be a contestant on the show, *Jeopardy!* seems to support an outcome-based approach to equality—it ensures the same outcome (the possibility of becoming a contestant) for all those who satisfy a certain criterion: namely, successfully completing the application process. Nevertheless, it might be suggested that genuinely *meaningful* equality requires something like assuring all contestants the same "reward" for appearing on the show. If one assumes that all contestants have "given their all" while playing the game, then don't they all deserve the same compensation for having done so?

John Rawls (1921–2002), among others, argued that equality of outcome is undesirable insofar as it undermines the incentive for the more industrious and talented to utilize their abilities to the greatest extent and, in turn, to the greatest benefit of all. That position was also advocated centuries earlier by John Locke, who stated:

> God gave the world to men in common; but since he gave it them for their benefit, and the greatest conveniences of life they were capable to draw from it, it cannot be supposed he meant it should always remain common and uncultivated. He gave it to the use of the industrious and rational (and labour was to be his title to it), not to the fancy or covetousness of the quarrelsome and contentious." (*Two Treatises on Government*, Chapter 5)

However, while Locke suggested that any resulting inequality is legitimate because it helps to avoid "wasting" available resources, Rawls asserted that inequality of outcome is acceptable only to the extent that the resulting distribution of goods is beneficial to the "least-advantaged" in society. In other words, it's perfectly acceptable to allow some individuals to possess greater wealth than others, for example, so long as their doing so also improves the situation of the least-advantaged.

But any action that increases the wealth of some without improving the lot of the least-advantaged is illegitimate and unacceptable. Rawls's stipulation regarding benefitting the least-advantaged is intended to compensate for what he argues is the *arbitrary* distribution of natural talents and individual circumstances—for example, possessing a "natural" athletic ability or being born into a wealthy or well-connected family—benefits that are the consequence of a "natural lottery."

Others have argued that, regardless of whether equality of outcome is desirable, it's an unrealizable and, consequently, unrealistic goal—at least within the existing political-economic framework that characterizes contemporary industrialized liberal democracies. In other words, it is simply not possible to establish an environment in which all *Jeopardy!* contestants achieve the type of stunning success obtained by Ken Jennings or Brad Rutter.

The arguments of Rawls, Locke, and others, promote an *equality of opportunity*: equality is realized when all have access to comparable opportunities. The outcomes generated by those opportunities may—and likely will—differ, substantially in some or many cases. Equality of opportunity seems to be a foundational principle of *Jeopardy!* All applicants and, in turn, contestants are given an identical opportunity to succeed, within the confines of the show. The fact that some, such as Ken Jennings and Brad Rutter, achieve a degree of success that enormously exceeds that realized by all others does not undermine the extent to which equality of opportunity is secured.

Within the context of *Jeopardy!*, equality of opportunity seems very much concerned with *procedures*. It can reasonably be assumed that the contestant application process and the regulations governing contestants' behavior during the game are intended to help ensure that (at least with regard to matters that can be controlled by the show's producers) all individuals have an equal opportunity to become contestants and to be successful on the show.

A focus on procedures raises another important distinction: namely, between *formal* and *substantive* equality. Whereas formal equality is concerned with proclaiming—for example, in government legislation or game show rules—the equality of individuals, substantive equality seeks both the formal/official affirmation of equality *and* the establishment of concrete mechanisms to ensure its realization. In other words, substantive equality requires the satisfaction of certain conditions—such as transparency and the universal application of identical criteria in the contestant selection processes and decisions—the absence of which need not render impossible the realization of merely formal equality. The goal of substantive equality can thus itself be understood as a "procedure" insofar as achieving that goal will dictate what types of behaviors and activities are acceptable or unacceptable.

I Will Remind Contestants that They Must . . .

Like equality, *Jeopardy!* is characterized both by opportunities and constraints. Contestants have the opportunity to use their personal knowledge and efforts to secure a significant cash reward—in many respects, the quintessential "American dream" (the realization of which is, ironically, shepherded by a Canadian host).

Contestants' success is principally a function of the knowledge they possess and their reflexes, relative to those of their competitors. Yes, the categories of questions that emerge during the course of a given game may end up playing to certain contestants' strengths more so than they do to those of others; however, given that no contestant knows in advance the categories that will be used, there is, in theory, an equal chance that each contestant may benefit from the categories. It thus seems reasonable to suggest that all contestants are provided with an equal opportunity to exercise their knowledge and reflexes.

Simultaneously, contestants must adhere to certain rules when playing the game if they wish to be successful. They must "buzz in" in order to answer a question, and all answers must be in the form of a question in order to be acceptable (though that requirement does not ensure that the answer is correct). Those constraints are applied identically to all contestants.

Many have argued that equality can be meaningfully achieved only when opportunity is accompanied by constraint. The idea of a "level playing field" is grounded in the belief that constraints are required in order to ensure that all individuals possess a relatively equal opportunity when competing for a particular good—a public office, for example. The opportunity-constraint position is promoted by Rawls and manifests itself clearly in his "second principle" of justice, which states: "Social and economic inequalities are to satisfy two conditions: first, they are to be attached to offices and positions open to all under conditions of fair equality of opportunity, and second, they are to be to the greatest benefit of the least-advantaged members of society."[1]

Those two conditions nicely exhibit the relationship between opportunity, constraint, and equality. The first condition, which has been labeled the "fair equality of opportunity clause," necessitates that all citizens have an equal opportunity to secure any public office. Rawls adds the adjective "fair" in order to emphasize that it is not merely a formal equality that is expected—it's not enough merely to proclaim that "all citizens have an equal opportunity to secure any public office." Rather, there must be a genuine, practical (that is, substantive) equality of opportunity available.

The second condition, which Rawls labels the *difference principle*, decrees that any activity that contributes to inequality is legitimate only if it also improves the circumstances of the least-advantaged in society. There is no claim that such a constraint produces equality of outcome, only that it prohibits illegitimate increases in inequality.

However, Ronald Dworkin, among others, has argued that meaningful equality demands more than equal opportunity; rather, it requires equality of *resources*. In order for opportunities to be meaningful, individuals must have the tools needed to capitalize on them. If certain individuals possess a greater number of those tools or have greater access to them than do others, then equality of opportunity is undermined. Only when individuals are provided with approximate equality of relevant resources—Rawls, for example, refers to "primary goods" such as income, wealth, freedom of movement, and the rights and liberties covered by the rule of law—can it reasonably be argued that meaningful equality is possible.

The idea of equality of resources highlights the relationship between equality and *responsibility*. Equality of resources neither assures nor demands equality of outcome. People with the

---

[1] John Rawls, *Justice as Fairness: A Restatement*, Belknap Press, 2001, pp. 42–43.

same resources will make different decisions as to how they use those resources, and those decisions will generate different outcomes. So, if a contestant on *Jeopardy!* chooses a category or places a wager that turns out to be detrimental—say, it causes that person to lose the game—many would argue that the resulting "unequal" outcome of the game is a consequence of a voluntary personal decision, and therefore is acceptable: the person is, in effect, responsible for the outcome.

By providing all individuals with relatively comparable means (that is, resources) that they can use to capitalize on opportunities to pursue and realize voluntarily determined goals, equality of resources is said to address a noteworthy deficiency associated with equality of opportunity while also offering the additional benefit of requiring that people accept responsibility for how they use the resources and opportunities they are provided.

I'm Sorry, but the Judges Have Ruled Your Answer Incorrect

Though there have been various attempts to "export" *Jeopardy!* beyond the United States, they have usually involved a modification to the way the game is played and, in turn, failed to gain or maintain sufficient popularity to remain on air for any extended period of time. Only in the United States has *Jeopardy!* achieved lasting success. But that fact poses an important challenge to the ability of the show to secure equality.

Philosopher Will Kymlicka has argued that meaningful equality—and, by extension, justice—requires that individuals' cultures be respected and protected. In order for individuals to make free and informed decisions about which path to pursue in life (an activity essential to human dignity), they must be able to draw upon understandings of "the good" as promoted by the beliefs and values that animate their ancestral culture, if so desired. To remove that possibility is to deny, among other things, an equal opportunity to be the architect of our decisions and actions; such a denial results in a failure to show equal respect for the individuals in question. So, according to this argument it's unjust to say that those who belong to dominant groups can enjoy the advantages and satisfactions of that membership, whereas those who belong to nondominant and minority groups must either abandon their culture or accept second-class status.

Kymlicka suggests that ensuring the necessary protection and respect may require establishing special provisions for certain groups. For example, it might be necessary to legislatively protect a certain language, as was the intention of Bill 101, The Charter of the French Language (*La charte de la langue française*), which made French the official language of Québec (Canada), while simultaneously restricting the official use of English in areas such as business, advertising, and education. Though such an action results in a system of *differentiated rights*—certain individuals or groups being granted rights not provided to other individuals or groups in society—it's nevertheless justifiable and, by extension, legitimate according to Kymlicka.

It might be argued that the knowledge that will enable contestants to be successful on *Jeopardy!* is, to an overwhelming extent, American-centric. Insofar as that's true, it undermines the equalitarian character of the show by generating a situation in which persons who were born and have spent their entire life in the United States are more likely to possess greater relevant knowledge—with regard to the questions that will be asked—than those who do not have such a lineage.

How might the producers of *Jeopardy!* effectively respond to such a challenge? One rebuttal that immediately springs to mind is to note that it is unfeasible to propose that *Jeopardy!* accommodate the entire range of cultural-linguistic diversity that exists in the United States. Not only would there be substantial costs associated with doing so, but altering the show in such a manner would likely have a drastic impact on its popularity and, consequently, its continued viability. However, Kymlicka does not propose that all cultures necessarily be assured equal protection. Rather, he distinguishes between "national minorities" and "ethnic minorities"—between minority cultures present at the founding of the nation, and those whose presence is the result of post-founding immigration—and concludes that the former have a stronger (and perfectly legitimate) claim to such protection.

Yet, even if one finds Kymlicka's argument ineffective in terms of critically undermining *Jeopardy!*'s equalitarian character, other challenges can be raised. In particular, Amartya Sen and Martha Nussbaum have both argued that meaningful equality requires focusing on individuals' *capabilities* when considering the type and distribution of resources provided to citizens for the pursuit and achievement of self-determined ends. People's capabilities may differ in terms of their health, knowledge, and wealth, among other things, and those differences will often have a noteworthy impact on their ability to take advantage of opportunities made available to them.

For example, providing a specific opportunity—say, the opportunity to make use of the facilities available at a local recreation center—to a person with a significant physical or cognitive disability may entail a cost that is substantially greater than that associated with providing the same opportunity to a person who does not suffer from such a physical or cognitive disability. However, according to the capabilities approach, meaningful equality requires that both be provided such an opportunity and the means needed to take advantage of it. Contestants playing *Jeopardy!* must "buzz in" in order to answer a question. But that means that individuals who are unable to operate the necessary equipment successfully are denied an equal opportunity to become contestants, as least in terms of how the show currently operates.

The "capabilities approach" affirms the belief that *equality* is not synonymous with *sameness*: to proclaim that two people are "equal" is not to say that they are identical. Rather, equality suggests that in at least one important respect—for example, their humanity or their capacity to suffer or their desire to pursue and realize a conception of the good life of their own design—they are alike, even though they might be different in many other ways. By establishing separate contestant categories (kids, teens, college students, adults, champions), *Jeopardy!* could be said to support an equality that recognizes different capabilities.

Sen, Nussbaum, and others would likely argue that such an accommodation does not sufficiently satisfy the demands of the capabilities approach. But as with the Kymlickian criticism, the producers of *Jeopardy!* might respond that it's unreasonable to expect the show to accommodate all possible circumstances that might arise were we to use a capabilities framework to determine the character of the competition. Yet, as with all rebuttals of this kind, it raises the question: at what point does providing equal concern and respect cost too much?

And the Answer Is, "Possibly"

Does *Jeopardy!* satisfy the demands of equality? The many definitions of equality that have emerged across the millennia have, in turn, generated an enormous range of suggestions concerning how we may best realize the conditions needed to achieve "meaningful" equality.

Looking at *Jeopardy!* as a case study in equality helps to demonstrate the complexity and essential contestability of the idea. But such an examination does not provide a definitive answer to the question of whether *Jeopardy!* satisfies the demands of equality. Moreover, history suggests that it's unlikely that such an answer exists or can ever be provided.

As Isaiah Berlin pointed out, there's no getting away from the fact that there will always be many different, often conflicting, values and beliefs, which cannot be rank-ordered in a way that would be acceptable to everyone. And so we must expect and accept that people will disagree about many things, especially something as important as what constitutes equality. That fact means that inequality will always exist.

And, as a spectator sport, *Jeopardy!* seems most exciting and engaging when there's some limited degree of "inequality" between the contestants—without such inequality we would likely never witness the thrill of a seventy-four-game winning streak by the likes of Ken Jennings.

3

What Makes *Jeopardy!* a Good Game?

BRENDAN SHEA

Jeopardy! occupies a special place among television game shows. Part of the reason for this undoubtedly has to do with simple longevity—with short interruptions, it has been on television since 1964—but this is hardly the only factor. A far more important difference between *Jeopardy!* and many other popular game shows involves their differing nature as *games*, and what it takes to play and win these games.

Winning consistently at *Jeopardy!*, unlike winning on other shows, requires considerable skill, and many of us admire those who demonstrate this skill. Ken Jennings, for example, was invited on late-night talk shows and given book deals in recognition of his long winning streak, and a computer (Watson) beating Jennings several years later was widely recognized as an indicator of how far artificial intelligence had progressed. It's hard to imagine similar reactions to a successful contestant (whether computer or human) on *Wheel of Fortune* or *Let's Make a Deal*.

Jeopardy! isn't the only game show that requires skill. Some of the dozens of quiz shows that have been on TV over the past four decades have, no doubt, been "tougher" to win than *Jeopardy!*, at least in terms of having more difficult questions or requiring players to obey more stringent rules. However, the skills required in *Jeopardy!*, unlike the skills required for many of these quiz shows, extend beyond mere knowledge of trivia. Successful *Jeopardy!* players must be good at such things as 1. using their knowledge of language to take advantage of the puns and humor that characterize *Jeopardy!* questions, 2. basing their wagers on good estimates of how likely their guesses are to be correct, and 3. predicting how their opponents will play.

Part of what makes *Jeopardy!* so distinctive is that it, unlike so many other TV game shows, is a genuinely good *game*. This presents a bit of a philosophical puzzle, however, as it can be difficult to pin down what exactly a *game* is. This difficulty has led some famous philosophers, including sometimes *Jeopardy!* category Ludwig Wittgenstein, to argue that it is actually impossible to provide a definition of *game* that isn't either too broad or too restrictive. Even more difficult, for us fans of good games, is to explain why it is that *Jeopardy!*'s being a good game even matters—after all, if you enjoy watching *Wheel of Fortune* and I enjoy watching *Jeopardy!*, it might seem that we merely have a difference of opinion on what counts as a good game, and that there is no fact of matter about who is right.

Many fans of *Jeopardy!* will no doubt have their favorite arguments at the ready ("You learn things watching the show!"), but the philosophical issues at stake—what does it mean to say that something is a *game,* what makes a game *good*, and why does that *matter?*—are deep ones worth considering in more detail.

How to Win at *Jeopardy!*

Becoming a *Jeopardy!* contestant (never mind a *Jeopardy!* winner) can be a laborious process. Potential candidates must take qualifying exams and screen tests, and then take time off work or school to fly out to Los Angeles if they are selected. Some of the most dedicated candidates might spend hundreds of hours on such tasks, including any studying they might decide to undertake. So, if all this effort is required, why do players do it? One reason might be for the hope of some reward, such as money, fame, or the self-confidence that comes with accomplishing something difficult. For many players, however, including the vast majority of us who will only ever play the

---

[1] In *Philosophical Investigations* Wittgenstein claims that while all games have a sort of "family resemblance" to one another, it isn't possible to define what it is that all games have in common.

video game or board game, it seems plausible that part of the reason for playing is for the sheer joy of it. This is typical of games, which are the sorts of activities people usually engage in for the sake of the activity itself, as opposed to activities like work that are done for some external purpose.

While individual *Jeopardy!* players might have a wide variety of personal reasons for competing, there is a sense in which all players have the *same* goals once the contest has started— they want to accumulate the available money and win the game. Again, this is typical of games, which are by their very nature a goal-directed activity.

With this in mind, a person might reasonably ask: "What's the goal of *Jeopardy!*, when we leave aside consideration of individual players, and think about it simply as a game?" This question might be answered in at least two ways:

1. **The goal is to have the most money at the end of show.**

2. **The goal is to win the game.**

While these goals might sound like two ways of describing the same thing, there are important differences between them that will prove crucial to our understanding of games.

The first goal, which we'll call the *prelusory goal*, is the end result that players must produce if they are to win, but is itself not the same thing as "winning the game." One might reach the prelusory goal by means fair (being knowledgeable and making wise wagers) or foul (blackmailing Alex for the answers—which take the form of questions—ahead of time).

In the former case, the player has also achieved the second goal, which consists in winning the game. In the latter case, however, it does not seem that the player has done this. In order to truly "win" a game, one must not only achieve the prelusory goal, but also do so in the right manner—by following rules. It wouldn't do, for instance, to bribe the skorekeeper to "accidentally" add $10,000 to your score before Final Jeopardy! (and then hope that no one notices).

Every game has a prelusory goal. For example, in Uno, one's prelusory goal is to get rid of all the cards, while in golf the prelusory goal is to get a small white ball in a hole. As these examples suggest, achieving the prelusory goal might well require the use of equipment that is normally used for games (such as Uno cards or golf clubs), or the exploitation of institutions that were originally designed with games in mind (such as TV shows on which players can win money). However, the prelusory goal exists independently of the game as such, and such goals can always (in principle, at least) be achieved without ever playing the game. For a concrete example of how this might be possible in a game like *Jeopardy!*, consider the contestants on the rigged quiz shows of the 1950s (made famous again by the movie *Quiz Show*), who apparently had goals very similar to the prelusory goals pursued by *Jeopardy!* contestants. They achieved these goals, however, not by playing a game but by following a script. *Jeopardy!* contestants who cheat are, in effect, doing something similar—they're achieving the prelusory goal of *Jeopardy!* without ever really playing the game.

The second goal, which we'll call the *lusory goal*, is achieved when a contestant reaches the prelusory goal of *Jeopardy!* by following the rules. In *Jeopardy!*, the contestant who "wins fair and square" has achieved the lusory goal. The lusory goal is both *complex,* in that it requires achieving the prelusory goal, and game-dependent, in that it cannot be achieved without playing the game of *Jeopardy!*. Just as every game has a prelusory goal, each game will also have a lusory goal that consists of achieving the prelusory goal in the right way.

Prelusory and lusory goals are not unique to *Jeopardy!*. In fact, leaving aside metaphorical uses of the word *game,* such as "the game of life" or "language games," these two distinct sorts of goals may very well exist for every game.

In his book *The Grasshopper*, Bernard Suits convincingly argues that nearly every game has a prelusory and lusory goal, and these two goals feature prominently in the definition of *game* he proposes (a definition we'll adopt here as well). Suits recognizes that a game is more than what it takes to win it, however. In addition to goals, every game must also have rules, and rules of a very particular type.

---

[2] Bernard Suits, *The Grasshopper: Games, Life, and Utopia* (University of Toronto Press, 1978).

Rules, Rules, and More Rules

The rules in *Jeopardy!*, just like rules in other games, come in several varieties. The first sort of rules prohibit players from pursuing the prelusory goal—the goal of having the most money at the end of the Final Jeopardy! round—in certain sorts of ways. So, for example, these rules stipulate that players aren't allowed to look up answers on their mobile phones, call their high school history teachers for advice, or supplement their total score by handing the scorekeeper some extra money they brought to the studio in their pockets.

Following Suits, we'll call the first sort of rules *constitutive rules*, since these rules constitute, or make up, a game. In *Jeopardy!*, some of the more easily recognizable constitutive rules include:

1. **All answers must be phrased in the form of a question,**

2. **Players can't ring in before Alex has finished reading the question, and**

3. **Players must determine their wager for Final Jeopardy! before they see the question (which, again, is in the form of an answer).**

These aren't the only constitutive rules of *Jeopardy!*, of course, and many of the constitutive rules deal with issues that rarely arise during a normal game. So, for example, the constitutive rules forbid players from using any kind of external aid, whether this be computer or human. Presumably, there are also general rules of conduct that forbid players from doing things like throwing their shoes at opponents in attempts to distract them.

Violations of constitutive rules will generate some sort of penalty. So, for example, if a contestant forgets to phrase his answer in the form of a question during Double Jeopardy! or Final Jeopardy!, the answer will count as incorrect. By contrast, if a contestant on the show were found to have an earpiece through which her aunt was feeding her answers, she would (presumably) forfeit the game.

By now, you probably have a pretty good sense of what counts as a constitutive rule of *Jeopardy!*. However, we still haven't given a definition of "constitutive rule," which is what we really need to do (as you read this book, you'll no doubt notice that philosophers love to provide definitions). We'll say that a *constitutive rule* is a rule that prohibits the players of a game from using certain means to achieve the prelusory goal, and thereby makes achieving the prelusory goal more challenging than otherwise would be the case. In other words, the constitutive rules make the players pursue the prelusory goal using means that are *inefficient.* Without the sorts of prohibitions introduced by constitutive rules, games such as *Jeopardy!* couldn't exist, since there would be no such thing as the lusory goal of winning by following the rules.

Constitutive rules aren't the only rules relevant to understanding *Jeopardy!*. A second sort of rules, which might be called *rules of thumb,* is also involved. Some sample rules of thumb (though not necessarily good ones) might be:

1. **A contestant who has less than $0 during the final moments of the Double Jeopardy! round should attempt to ring in aggressively.**

2. **The first-place contestant in Final Jeopardy! should never wager more than needed to win, and**

3. **Players should always answer "Who is Martin van Buren?" for any question about a US president that stumps them.**

As these examples should make clear, rules of thumb, unlike constitutive rules, aren't really essential to understanding the nature of *Jeopardy!* as a game. Rather, rules of thumb relate to the difference between good *Jeopardy!* players (who use well-founded rules of thumb) and bad ones (the ones who guess "Martin van Buren" more than they perhaps should). The question of what makes a good *Jeopardy!* player, while certainly an interesting one, isn't as fundamental as the ones we'll be trying to answer. It concerns the *way* we ought to play games (if we want to win) rather than *what* games are and *why* we bother playing them at all.

There is another sort of rules that sometimes become relevant to game playing—the moral and legal rules that govern our conduct in general. These rules prohibit, among other things, attempting to win *Jeopardy!* by murder, blackmail, or theft. While I haven't checked, my guess is that breaking one of these rules probably violates the regulations agreed to by potential contestants on *Jeopardy!*. If this is true, this is a happy coincidence, since there are certainly some games (from backroom poker to illegal street fights) where following the constitutive rules of the game is no guarantee that one is following other, more important, rules.

Please Answer in the Form of a Question

All of this talk about constitutive rules might seem pretty obvious—after all, you can't have a game without rules, right? But there's a deeper point here as well. The constitutive rules governing games are, in certain very important ways, completely unlike the rules that govern the rest of our lives, such as the legal and moral prohibitions just mentioned.

Consider, for instance, the well-known *Jeopardy!* rule that requires players to answer in the form of a question. This rule, like every good constitutive rule, is designed to introduce an element of inefficiency and, thus, challenge. For the very same reasons that answering in the form of a question makes a good constitutive rule for a game, it would make a terrible rule for life in general. It would certainly make ordering at restaurants a challenge ("What is the bacon double cheeseburger?"), and cause absolute havoc when used to respond to marriage proposals ("What is 'yes'?"), to name just a couple of examples. Where a little forced inefficiency can make the pursuit of the prelusory goals of games all the more interesting and worthwhile, the same can hardly be said of life goals in general. For goals like obtaining nourishment and finding love, people tend (with good reason!) to favor the means that allows them to most efficiently achieve their goals.

This contrast highlights what is perhaps the deepest difference between the constitutive rules of games and the moral and legal rules governing our conduct in general—namely, the reason that we obey them. While there's no generally accepted account of why we ought to follow moral and legal rules, one can imagine any number of plausible answers: "Because people won't associate with me if I don't," "Because I don't want to go to jail," "Because moral people tend to be happier," "Because it's the right thing to do." These sorts of answers are not available for the constitutive rules of games, however. In games like *Jeopardy!*, the reason that players obey the constitutive rules is that 1. you can't play *Jeopardy!* without obeying the constitutive rules and 2. the players want to play *Jeopardy!*. The reason we follow constitutive rules is because we want to play the games they make possible, and not for any higher-minded reason.

With this reason for following constitutive rules in mind, we're finally ready to offer a definition of what a *game* is and get on with the business of explaining why *Jeopardy!* is a good game. A *game* is an activity that has each of the following:

1. **A prelusory goal, which is the game-independent result that the participants aim to accomplish.**

2. **One or more constitutive rules limiting the means to pursue this goal.**

3. **Participants who follow the constitutive rules for the reason that they want to participate in the activity. We'll call this attitude the *lusory attitude*.**

By these criteria, *Jeopardy!* is clearly a game, whereas, say, the typical commute to work is not. While commuting to work certainly has a goal (getting there), it isn't the sort of activity that has constitutive rules introducing deliberate inefficiencies (most of us don't drive our cars an extra lap around the block just to add time), and the average commuter doesn't have the requisite attitude (the reason she is traversing the distance to work isn't for the sake of covering the distance).

We can imagine a person who turned the daily commute into a game, for example, by deciding that she would aim to take at least one new street every day on her way to work. This adoption of a new constitutive rule, combined with the shift in attitude, might signal that her commute was no longer just about getting to work, but was also being done for its own sake. However, while this activity might qualify as a game, it hardly seems like the sort of game, à la *Jeopardy!*, that would be worth playing more than once or twice. This observation brings us to our next point—not all games are created equal.

Playing a Good Game

So far, we've explored what it means to claim that *Jeopardy!* is a game, and in doing so have also provided an account of what games are in general. Merely showing that *Jeopardy!* is a game doesn't do much for us, though, unless we can draw a meaningful distinction between good games and bad games and explain why it is that good games matter.

Many of the characteristics that make *Jeopardy!* a better game than other television game shows probably seem self-evident (or at least, they probably seem self-evident to fans of *Jeopardy!*). I talked a little about these characteristics earlier: *Jeopardy!* is challenging, success involves skill as opposed to pure luck, and the skills *Jeopardy!* requires (like general purpose knowledge, a good betting strategy, and the ability to predict what your opponents will do) are good life skills. This suggests that a large part of what separates good games from not-so-good games is what they require of those who play. Playing a good game well—whether it be *Jeopardy!*, chess, or basketball—requires that we do more than simply show up and hope for the best. We have to dig down, try hard, and use the skills we've developed to meet the challenges presented by the game.

Just as when we were searching for the definition of a *game*, though, we'll have to be careful if we want to figure out the difference between good games and games. The comparison between *Jeopardy!* and game shows like *Wheel of Fortune* suggests that part of the difference has to do with difficulty—a good game should be *difficult*, in the sense that winning the game requires the players to challenge themselves in significant ways. However, it also won't do to simply say that the best games are the *most* difficult ones. After all, we could imagine a revised version of *Jeopardy!* in which a contestant won only if she got every question correct, with the game otherwise being declared a draw and none of the players being invited to come back to play again the next day. We could devise an infinite number of progressively sillier constitutive rules along these lines—one could require that players ring in within 0.1 second of hearing the clue read, that they express their answers in questions that were exactly 140 characters in length, or that they juggle a set of steak knives throughout the *Jeopardy!* contest.

This suggests that a good game must have a set of constitutive rules that strike a successful balance between 1. making reaching the prelusory goal too easy, where winning requires little or no effort, and 2. making reaching the prelusory goal so insanely difficult that players may as well not bother trying. Games whose rules are either too loose or too strict will create a situation where players don't have any motivation to exert their best effort in winning the game. In good games, unlike in bad games, winning is not merely a matter of luck.[3] Even a casual fan knows that winning *Jeopardy!* involves some luck, especially with respect to the questions that happen to be posed.

Over the years, *Jeopardy!* has undergone a number of revisions to its rules that reflect the importance of maintaining this balance. So, for example, when *Jeopardy!* first aired, players were allowed to buzz in at any time they so desired, even if the question was still being read. This rule risked creating a situation where speed with the buzzer was doing more to help players win than knowledge of *Jeopardy!* questions or wise betting strategy. Because it was (rightly) felt that *Jeopardy!* would be a better game if winning depended more on knowledge, the constitutive rules of *Jeopardy!* were revised to ensure that players could not buzz in before the question had been read (and, if they violated this rule by attempting to buzz in early, their buzzer would be "locked out" for a short time afterward).

What Good Games Are Good For

If everything I've said so far is accurate, then we're finally in a place to claim with confidence that *Jeopardy!* is a good game. First of all, it's a game with a prelusory goal (getting the most money), constitutive rules (such as answering in the form of question), and participants who are in it for the right reasons (because they want to play *Jeopardy!*). Second, it's a *good* game—a game in which the constitutive rules strike a successful balance between making winning too difficult and too easy. We still haven't looked at the really important question, though: why does the fact that *Jeopardy!* is a good game matter, anyway?

---

[3] Robert Simon has written about the role of luck in games in "Deserving to Be Lucky: Reflections on the Role of Luck and Desert in Sports," *Journal of the Philosophy of Sport* (May 2007).

One straightforward answer to this question might simply note that, since good games challenge players to show determination, dedication, and skill, they are for that very reason good things. All other things being equal, challenging activities such as *Jeopardy!* are simply more worthwhile than activities that require no effort whatsoever.

A second reason for suggesting that good games matter involves the *instrumental value* of the skills they help players develop. Many of the skills required by *Jeopardy!*—general knowledge, the ability to think quickly, and so on—have clear relevance for the lives of players outside of the game. This idea is a very intuitive one, and it is one that is often made by defenders of the value of games and sports. Randolph Feezell, a philosopher who writes on the value of sports, has discussed the role that sports (which are simply a type of game) play in developing the sort of *character* that proves valuable for other life activities.[4]

While this purely instrumental function of good games is no doubt important, it would be a mistake to conclude that *Jeopardy!* is valuable for the sole reason that it is educational. After all, part of the reason that people enjoy watching and playing games is precisely to get away from the "real world" where every activity has to have some definite purpose. People play games because they are fun, and it would be surprising and disappointing if the value of *Jeopardy!* depended entirely on how much use you got out of the various facts that you managed to memorize when you were watching the show.

Two final reasons for good games mattering have been suggested by Thomas Hurka and John Tasioulas.[5] The first is that playing a good game well amounts to an objectively valuable accomplishment. This objective value is rooted in the fact that playing a good game well requires that players accomplish a wide variety of small tasks. So, for example, winning a game of *Jeopardy!* against skilled opponents requires that a player answer a large number of questions correctly, bet wisely, and stay focused enough to ring in at the right time. It's precisely because playing *Jeopardy!* well requires this varied combination of smaller accomplishments that it is more objectively

[4] Randolph Feezell, *Sport, Play, and Ethical Reflection,* University of Illinois Press, 2006.
[5] "Games and the Good." *Proceedings of the Aristotelian Society* (2006).

valuable than, say, being the winning contestant on *Let's Make a Deal*, which demands far less of contestants.

Hurka and Tasioulas's second reason for thinking that games are valuable has to do with the lusory attitude possessed by game players. This attitude involves the fact that game players (unlike participants in many other activities) must voluntarily adopt the (inefficient) rules of the game for the reason that *they want to play the game.* Hurka and Tasioulas argue that this attitude, which consists of wanting to a do a good thing for the very properties that make it good, is itself a good thing. Again, the fact that this sort of attitude is a good thing should make sense upon reflection. A deserving person's being happy, for instance, is a thing that most of us would recognize as a good thing. The idea here is that a second person's finding joy in that deserving person's happiness is also a good thing. So, if playing a challenging game like *Jeopardy!* is objectively good, then so is the fact that *Jeopardy!* players do so (at least in part) because they want to play a challenging game.

You Can (and Should) Play Along at Home!

People watch *Jeopardy!* for many reasons—they enjoy the humor, they learn things, they just enjoy watching the competition, and so on. At least part of the fun for many of us, though, is the sense that we can "play along" with the contestants on TV by seeing how quickly we can think of the correct answers and considering how we would bet in various situations. This sort of active watching itself counts as a sort of game, with a prelusory goal (get the question correct before the contestant does!) and various constitutive rules (no looking at your cell phone!). Moreover, it's an activity whose rules we obey precisely because we find the activity worthwhile and we want to participate in it.

While the challenges presented by these simpler, solitary games hardly rise to the level of flying out to California to compete on *Jeopardy!*, they're a reminder that almost all of us are game players at one point or another, and that our lives are enriched by good games like *Jeopardy!*[6]

---

[6] Thanks to everyone who read and gave comments on drafts of this article: Adam Bowen, Anne Rumery, Anne Shea, Eric Schaaf, Joe Swenson, Rachel Brito, and Uwe Plebuch.

4
Cliff Lost on *Jeopardy!*, Baby

FRANKLIN ALLAIRE

Anyone who watches *Jeopardy!*, whether it's on a regular basis or as a fair-weather fan, goes through a range of emotions as the show progresses. There is a seething undercurrent of disappointment that Alex Trebek, who's hosted *Jeopardy!* since 1984, shaved off his mustache in 2001 (facial hair enthusiasts flew their goatees at halfstaff on that day). The rest of us feel frustration, disbelief, amazement, and probably a little bit of jealousy towards the contestants who seem to know everything about everything! After all, how many of us can rattle off facts ranging from different countries' national holidays to 1940s trivia, to words that start with "Kh", all in the span of mere seconds?

The twenty-eight Trebek seasons of *Jeopardy!* have seen their fair share of amazing contestants. Seventy-four-time *Jeopardy!* champion Ken Jennings holds the all-time record for the most wins and winnings with over three million dollars in regular competition—not including *Jeopardy!* specials such as millionaire's rounds, tournaments of champions, celebrity or college editions. "Moneyballer" Roger Craig used a computer program to analyze and study patterns in questions and now holds the record for the most money won in a single game. Then there's Watson, a room-sized IBM question-answering machine that demonstrated advances in artificial intelligence: Watson could understand questions posed in natural language and answer them (I, too, welcome our new computer overlords!).

He's the Harbinger of Postmodernism

Jeopardy!'s staying power and pop-culture influence (*Saturday Night Live*'s take on *Celebrity Jeopardy!* is a hilarious case-in-point) cannot be denied. However, its very successful answer-question format is challenged by postal worker, resident barfly, and self-proclaimed know-it-all Cliff Clavin (John Ratzenberger) in one of my favorite episodes of *Cheers* appropriately entitled "What Is Cliff Clavin?"

In an appearance on *Jeopardy!* Cliff calls in to question the fundamental single-question answer foundation of *Jeopardy!* with his humorous yet "incorrect" response, "Who are three people who've never been in my kitchen?," to the clue "Archibald Leach, Bernard Schwartz, and Lucille LeSueur." The "correct" response was "What are the real names of Cary Grant, Tony Curtis, and Joan Crawford?" I think we can all thank them for changing their names!

Is Cliff's insistence that his response is correct a desperate plea from a sore loser? Probably. No one likes to be wrong, especially when we're on television and have marketed ourselves to friends as the purveyor of annoyingly useless and barely reliable trivia, the way Cliff has. Adding insult to injury, Cliff's success during the first two rounds of *Jeopardy!* left him with $22,000 all of which he wagers and loses on his "incorrect" answer. The winner was crowned with a measly $400. This has given rise to what's known on *Jeopardy!* as *Clavin's Rule:* When in first place, you should never wager enough to endanger a "lock" or "runaway" game, no matter how tempting the category might be.

On the other hand, could Cliff be channeling postmodern philosophy in an attempt to challenge the very nature of *Jeopardy!* itself? Probably not. However, Cliff's hilariously "incorrect" answer raises some philosophical issues regarding both modern and postmodern theories of knowledge.

I believe that not only was Cliff's answer wrong, it was ridiculously wrong and he lost fair and square. Unlike *Jeopardy!* contestants, we don't have to worry about buzzing in and forming a question in fifteen seconds or less. Therefore, we have the luxury of exploring a major philosophical concept—knowledge (aka epistemology)—and how it relates to two competing schools of philosophical thought: modernism and postmodernism.

Epistemology (the theory of knowledge) explores the formation and scope of knowledge. Modernism, from a philosophical standpoint, is the tendency in contemporary culture and society to accept only "objective" truth. Modernism is rooted in the scientific, technological, artistic, and philosophical transformation of society during the 1890s and early 1900s. Postmodernism can be understood as a result, reaction, aftermath, denial, or rejection of modernism. Postmodern philosophy is a school of thought which proposes that reality is more complex and dynamic than suggested by the objectivity of modernism, because reality is socially constructed and therefore subject to change.

While epistemology is concerned with distinguishing genuine from bogus knowledge, who or what determines what counts as "genuine" knowledge and truth, and whether that knowledge is truly objective, is at the heart of the modern-postmodern debate. Cliff's "wrong" response challenges *Jeopardy!*'s notion that there is one and only one question for each answer given, just as postmodern philosophy challenges modernist assumptions. Therefore, Cliff could find himself in the company of postmodern philosophers such as Ernest Becker, Gilles Deleuze, and Michel Foucault, who have sought to challenge modernist assumptions regarding knowledge and societal norms by deconstructing socially and culturally constructed symbols, macro- and micro-level differences, and self-perpetuating power structures, respectively.

I'll Take "Knowing What We Know" for $500 Alex!

Before we can explore how knowledge is approached from both modern and postmodern perspectives, we need to have a basic understanding of what knowledge is. Epistemologists (yes, that's a real word and you'll probably see it on Final Jeopardy! one day) take several different approaches to knowledge. In general, and in this chapter, the kind of knowledge usually discussed is *propositional knowledge*, or *knowledge that*—something that can be expressed in a statement or sentence that describes a fact or a state of affairs. "Humans are mammals," "2 + 2 = 4," and "Disneyland is in California" are all examples of propositional knowledge.

Other types of knowledge are *knowledge how* and *acquaintance-knowledge*. For example, in the area of mathematics a *Jeopardy!* contestant needs only to know *that* πr^2 describes the area of a circle. He or she does not necessarily have to know *how* it describes the area of circle. In a mathematic class, however, not only is your *knowledge that* being tested, you also need to know *how* to multiply πr^2.

These two types of knowledge are, in turn, both different from *acquaintance-knowledge*, which focuses on the recognition of things, even if we don't necessarily know them or how they function. This includes knowing a *person* (He was the first Prime Minister of the United Kingdom under Queen Victoria[1]), a *place* (These are underwater sink holes commonly found in Belize, the Bahamas, and Australia[2]), a *thing* (This breed of dog was raised by lamas and kept as good luck charms and monastery watch dogs[3]), or an *activity* (This sport, in which players slide "stones" across ice towards a target area, has been in the Winter Olympics since 1998[4])

Legend has it that the idea for *Jeopardy!* was inspired by Merv Griffin's wife, who lamented that there had not been a really good trivia show on television since the quiz show scandals of the 1950s. Typically, quiz shows relied on a standard question-answer format—the host asked the question and the contestants tried to answer them correctly. *Jeopardy!*'s answer-question format turns that idea around and requires contestants to put propositional knowledge into the form of a question.

So in *Jeopardy!* we're not dealing so much with knowledge propositions. Instead we're dealing with *knowledge interrogatives*—a fact or state of affairs that can be expressed as a question. Thus the statement "The President of the United States lives in the White House" can be *Jeopardy!*-ized into the proposition "He lives in the White House" that leads to the knowledge interrogative "Who is the President of the United States?"; similarly, "The distance around a spherical object" leads to "What is circumference?"

---

[1] Who is Sir Robert Peel?
[2] What are blue holes?
[3] What is a Tibetan Terrier?
[4] What is curling?

In this way *Jeopardy!* becomes a great exercise in demonstrating what we know. It forces us to process and demonstrate *knowledge that* in a different way from what we're used to. It also illustrates all three types of knowledge in that we have to know what a question is (knowledge that), how to form a question (knowledge how), and when a particular question is appropriate (acquaintance-knowledge).

We can also distinguish between different types of propositional knowledge depending on where that knowledge comes from. On the one hand, non-empirical knowledge is usually referred to as *a priori*—meaning that knowledge is independent or *prior* to any experience that requires the use of reason. On the other hand, empirical or *a posteriori* knowledge is gained only after, or *posterior* to, experiences and the use of reason.

But where does knowledge come from? Why is some knowledge more important than other knowledge? What does it mean to know something? What's the difference between someone who knows something and someone who doesn't?

Our First Daily Double—Belief and Truth

For centuries, philosophers have been grappling with what knowledge is, where it comes from, and how we use it. Even Plato struggled with the issue in several of his dialogues, including *Meno*, *Phaedrus*, and *Theaetetus*. In both *Meno* and *Phaedrus*, Socrates explains how the immortal soul has already learned everything prior to inhabiting the human body. All knowledge, therefore, is *inborn* and the best path towards recollection of this knowledge is through rhetoric and—wait for it—*Socratic* questioning (funny how that works).

We need to remember that knowledge is a specific kind of mental state that exists only in thinking animals. Knowledge and our ability to use it, especially to plan ahead and self-reflect, are seen as particularly important characteristics that make humans unique among the animal kingdom. Unthinking things can't know anything. And while *knowledge that* propositions can be used to describe aspirations, desires, and intentions, they do not *necessarily* constitute knowledge. Knowledge itself is a kind of belief. If one has no beliefs about something, one cannot have any knowledge of it.

In *Theaetetus*, Socrates examines several theories concerning what knowledge is and develops a definition of knowledge as *justified true belief*—in order to know that a given proposition is true, one must not only believe the relevant truth in the proposition but also have a good reason for doing so. In other words, I can believe something that may or may not be true but I can't *know* if it's true or not unless I have a justification for doing so.

This adds some weight to Cliff's argument that his answer is correct. Not only does he *believe* that Archibald Leach, Bernard Schwartz, and Lucille LeSueur have never been in his kitchen, there may be some justification because he claims to *know* that they have not been in his kitchen! At least we can assume he knows because it is, after all, his kitchen. In fact, at the conclusion of the *Jeopardy!* taping Cliff proceeds to rattle off the names of other people who he believes to have never been in his kitchen.

However, just because we believe something is a truth does not ensure that it is really true. Human history is full of examples in which "true believers" affirm a particular belief regardless of whether evidence suggests that said belief is a "true" representation of the issue in question. Switch on your TV to the talking heads of various cable news networks and you'll see plenty of examples of beliefs devoid of truth or, even worse, passing for truths. Just imagine trying to keep score in a game where all of the contestants *knew* they were correct because they *believed* they were correct.

So knowledge requires belief, but not all beliefs constitute knowledge. While some of our beliefs are true, others are false. As we seek knowledge, we're essentially trying to increase our volume of *true and valid* beliefs that we posses, while minimizing the false ones. This is one of the greatest challenges faced by teachers in classrooms around the world—not only creating belief but also exchanging students' false beliefs with those that are true.

There are lots of reasons why we create beliefs. Cultural anthropologist and philosopher Ernest Becker cites the need to create order in a chaotic universe, seek a match between one's mind and the world, and create a positive image of oneself and others, as the primary motivations.[5] But when we seek knowl-

---

[5] *The Birth and Death of Meaning*, second edition, The Free Press, 1971.

edge, we're trying to get things right! This creates problems for us because our beliefs and the truth about the world around us don't always match. Truth, is a condition of knowledge. But how do we determine if something is true?

Our Second Daily Double—Justification and Objectivity

Because of luck, a belief can be unjustified yet true; and because of human fallibility, a belief can be justified yet false. Slowly but surely Socratic notions of knowledge as belief were picked apart as scientific theories, experiments, and discoveries replaced subjective beliefs with objective truths throughout the Enlightenment era of the eighteenth and nineteenth centuries. While scientists were picking apart beliefs to get to truth physically, heavy-hitting philosophers such as René Descartes and Immanuel Kant were picking them apart metaphysically.

Descartes stressed that subjective reality is better known than objective reality. However, he felt that objective knowledge of one's reality was just as basic as the subjective reality we each experience. To him, knowledge started with the immediate knowledge of one's subjective states and proceeds to the objective knowledge of one's own existence as a thinking thing: *Cogito, ergo sum* (I think, therefore I am)—we infer our own existence from the subjective reality of our own thinking. All objective knowledge, according to Descartes, rests on this immediate knowledge of one's own existence as a thinking thing. Accordingly, all *Jeopardy!* categories would be unique to you and based on something that you've personally experienced.

In Kant's *Prolegomena to Any Future Metaphysics*, he expresses concerns over subjective lines of thinking. He uses the phrase *Ding an sich* (the thing-in-itself) to designate pure objectivity as being independent of the features of any subjective perception of it. The scientific method, which we'll all remember from high-school science classes, was becoming codified at the time; it was an attempt to systematically understand the nature of things as they appear to us. This involved accurate and precise measurements that allegedly enabled scientists to reach objective judgments—judgments having a high probability of expressing truth regarding a reality. For instance, two people giving differing reports about the weather (chilly versus pleasant) illustrates the variation in judgments and is an indicator of subjectivity. Measurements of temperature (20°C) are often taken to indicate a level of objectivity. Philosophers usually refer to this as *intersubjective agreement*.

Does intersubjective agreement prove objective truth? No. Just because two or three people agree that it's cold outside doesn't preclude the possibility that someone else might find it pleasant. What if there was intersubjective agreement among a large number of subjects? This line of reasoning appears promising, except that it's more like the "truthiness" Stephen Colbert and countless political pundits have made infamous. Along these lines, Cliff's response could be judged a correct response if one of the other two contestants (a simple majority) verified that those three particular individuals had never been in Cliff's kitchen.

Modernity's goal, in terms of knowledge, is to utilize science and technology to obtain and understand the *most* objective knowledge possible. We accomplish this by finding more and more ways to remove ourselves from the things we study. This has driven scientific advances in technology to measure things more accurately and reliably even at the nano-, pico-, and femto- levels to better understand the reality in which we live. Technology has given us the ability to peer into the farthest reaches of space, explore the inner workings of our DNA, and explain physical, chemical, and biological phenomena. According to Kant, the quest for objective knowledge is really the search for the perfect *universal* intersubjective agreement. But is such a thing possible?

At times, it certainly seems that way. The late-nineteenth and twentieth centuries have come to be known as the age of modernity—a reality in which science and technology, including the use of mass communication and transportation, has reshaped human perceptions. In this reality, science has sought to distinguish itself from the narrative knowledge of place-based tribal wisdom communicated through myths, legends, and experience (knowledge *how*) by emphasizing information as a mean rather than an end.

As we've moved to a more scientific and technologically driven society, we rely less on subjective judgments and more on objective measurements that can be tested, retested, falsified, and proved. With knowledge available at our fingertips any-where in the world 24/7, the world has gotten appreciably smaller and we, as a species, have gotten more culturally similar. While *Jeopardy!* itself could have been viewed as exclusively American in the 1960s and early-1970s, it is now distributed internationally and airs across the world. Adaptations of *Jeopardy!* are aired in almost thirty different countries and their champions are occasionally invited to compete in international *Jeopardy!* tournaments in the United States. While their own hosts may lack Alex Trebek's trademark wit and charm, you're just as likely to hear them offer up a "Potpourri" of trivia in Israel and the Arab World, Estonia, and Argentina.

Here's the rub—human beings are subjective creatures. The inherent flaw with modernism is an assumption of objectivity. Modernism assumes that objective knowledge is the *only* correct knowledge regardless of age, ethnicity, gender, socioeconomic status, and sexual preference (just to name a few) and the reality or realities in which you live. Objective knowledge assumes that what's true for *one* group is true for *all* groups. If your reality doesn't match the universal intersubjective agreement that society has come to, then your conception of reality is just as wrong as your likely responses on *Jeopardy!* because your understanding of the issue at hand differs from the accepted "objective" truth.

Finding the Same Answers Through Different Questions

Insisting that only objective knowledge is genuine denies individual, group, and societal interpretations. Ernest Becker realized the importance of subjectivity in the human need to find meaning in a chaotic universe. How an individual defines, interprets and reacts to a symbol depends on the cultural significance of that symbol. Becker proposed that we measure our self-worth by our ability to live up to cultural standards. The challenge, he notes, is that different cultures have different standards of measurement.

Colors, images, animals, plants, and geographic locations might be significant to different cultures but for different reasons. The raven, for example, is a bird that can be viewed through several different cultural lenses: it's the creator and life-giver to Native Americans; a servant of Odin in Norse mythology; and an avatar of Bran the Blessed to the Celts. Postmodernism believes that reducing knowledge to separate non-intersecting categories (like those on a *Jeopardy!* board) dissolves the coherence of knowledge and causes it to lose its meaning entirely.

The loss of meaning in modernity results from preventing the interacting and intersecting of epistemology with two other broad concepts: axiology (how we relate to and derive value from knowledge personally, culturally, and existentially) and ontology (the nature of being, existence, and reality). Modernism's reliance on objective knowledge, therefore, becomes a source of power, which Alex Trebek wields with an iron fist.

Historian and postmodern philosopher Michel Foucault, who is most often credited with tackling power from the angle of knowledge as systems of thought that become controlling, socially legitimated, and institutional, notes that power is not something that some posses while others don't. Instead power, particularly knowledge, should be seen as a tactical and resourceful narrative that dominates our lives. We live it, rather than have it.[6]

I don't see *Jeopardy!*-type knowledge per se becoming a system of discourse that will eventually dominate us socially and culturally. Just imagine trying to order a coffee at Starbucks in the form of a question! However, Cliff's assertion that there exist different questions for the same answers sheds light on the lack of objectivity inherent in modernism's "objective" knowledge. In this way, Alex Trebek (as host) and the *Jeopardy!* judges become gatekeepers of knowledge and determine which knowledge is legitimate and which is to be excluded.

Let's say the *Final Jeopardy!* category is "History," and we're given the answer "Battles during this war from 1861 to 1865 took place exclusively on Southern US soil." The most obvious response would probably be "What is the American Civil War?" After all, that's what was written in our history textbooks (gatekeepers of knowledge). However, this is not the only term used for this particular war. Perhaps one of the

---

[6] *The Archaeology of Knowledge*, Vintage, 2010.

Jeopardy! contestants is a member of the Sons of Confederate Veterans and responds with "What is the Second American Revolution?", or "What is the War of Northern Aggression?", or "What is the War for Southern Independence?" Maybe one of the contestants insists on responding with "What is the War of Rebellion?" or "What is the War of Secession?" Additionally, one of the contestants could be the descendant of freed slaves and responds with "What is the Freedom War?" to celebrate the effect the war had on ending slavery in the United States.

Taken to a Cliff Clavin*esque* extreme, one could respond with "What is a war that did not involve Portugal?" or "What is a war in which I haven't fought?" Are all of these responses correct? Are any of them correct? Are none of them correct? Who decides?

What Is the Power of *Jeopardy!?*

On *Jeopardy!* the official judges determine the correct and incorrect answers. But what constitutes legitimate knowledge in the larger society is not as cut and dry as it would be during the Final Jeopardy! round. This is because the conventional expectation of history, and other subjects for that matter, is that they're something linear—a chronology of inevitable facts that tell a story that makes sense. This type of modernist perspective is false. Reality is much more complicated and is filled with underlayers of what is kept suppressed, oppressed, and unconscious in and throughout history.

Foucault's fellow French postmodernist Gilles Deleuze supports this vision of intersubjective agreement in which difference (and both real and existential disagreement) is subordinated by identity, opposition, and resemblance.[7] Our understanding of history, knowledge and ourselves is born out of a reflection from the imaginary. These imaginary reflections are both conscious and unconscious and can be sources of both real and existential dread when one compares the imaginary to reality. The power that *Jeopardy!* exerts on Cliff and other ridiculously wrong contestants does not reside in the dollar values of each category or in the wealth *Jeopardy!* champions accumulate. According to Foucault, *Jeopardy!*'s power is in its

---

[7] Deleuze, *Difference and Repetition*, Columbia University Press, 1994.

ability to control the narrative and therefore the reality that exists on each and every episode of the show.

By insisting that reality, and therefore knowledge, involves a network of differences, gradients, and overlaps, both Foucault and Deleuze upset the codes and assumptions of modernist order and their structures of exclusion that legitimate societal identities. According to Foucault and Deleuze, such differences should be appreciated for their own sake rather than criticized or viewed as "wrong" by society. They reveal that there is no "knowledge," only an interactive and intersecting series of legitimate vs. excluded *knowledges*.

This is all well and good in the "real" world. But *Jeopardy!*'s judges and, by extension, its host decide what is legitimate knowledge in the reality of the *Jeopardy!* universe. Not only do the judges determine the knowledge *that* contestants must know to win, they also determine the exact knowledge interrogatives they will need to use to express said knowledge. They make the rules. They guard the gates. They hold *all* of the keys.

We Have Some Lovely Parting Gifts for You...

While knowledges may result in the same answers, the questions we use to get there sprout from different realities in terms of gender, class, ethnicity, sexuality, culture, language, time period and even individual experiences (just to name a few). Postmodern identity is characterized by an emphasis on inner voice and the search for authentic knowledge in which an individual can find a way of being that is somehow true to themselves. All roads may lead to a "truth" (with a lower-case "t"), but not everyone takes the same roads. This reality places individual differences in a more positive light, looks positively on both inter- and intra-group differences, and creates a framework through which we can appreciate each other's inherent qualities.

Cliff's challenge to *Jeopardy!*'s answer-single question format opens the door to the acceptance that different knowledges and knowledge systems are just as valid as "accepted" knowledge. This is what makes him a true champion. And while I find it highly unlikely that the *Jeopardy!* producers will schedule a Postmodern Tournament of Champions in the foreseeable future, I'll keep my hand on the buzzer just in case.

I'll Take Slogans, Alex

Here are the Answers
(For the Questions, see page 187)

1. This Genevan philosopher proclaimed: "Man is born free; and everywhere he is in chains."

2. This literary duo is responsible for the rallying cry: "Workers of the world, unite. You have nothing to lose but your chains!"

3. Before going insane, he proclaimed: "What does not kill me makes me stronger."

4. This influential doctor advised 1960s young people to "Turn on, tune in, and drop out!"

5. This nineteenth-century liberal wrote: "All power tends to corrupt. Absolute power corrupts absolutely."

6. The claim that "all sex is rape" was attributed to her, though she disputed this interpretation of her writings.

7. He wrote: "That government is best which governs not at all."

8. "Existence comes before Essence" is the maxim of this philosophical movement.

9. This old saying, quoted in an 1855 poem by Browning, was made into a slogan of the new architecture by Ludwig Mies van der Rohe.

10. "The medium is the message," proclaimed this Canadian scholar.

11. This slogan voiced by Otto Liebman in 1865 rallied German philosophers opposed to absolute idealism.

12. "Freedom is slavery" is one of the three main slogans of this ruling political party.

13. This De Beers slogan is not true, since carbon crystals must eventually degrade to something like powdered graphite.

14. This value judgment is a fundraising tagline of the American Negro College Fund.

15. A maxim of Mao Zedong urges us to put this in command.

16. This politician's presidential campaign motto was "Tippecanoe and Tyler Too."

17. The 2008 Obama presidential campaign derived this English-language slogan from the Spanish-language motto of the United Farm Workers.

18. This successful Nike slogan was inspired by a remark of mass murderer Gary Gilmore.

19. This US president was the first to proclaim: "The Buck Stops Here."

20. This campaign slogan by supporters of 1884 presidential candidate James Blaine drew attention to the fact that their opponent Grover Cleveland had fathered an illegitimate child.

21. Maxwell House has attributed this slogan to a remark by Teddy Roosevelt, though some historians are not convinced.

22. He said that it is better to be "Socrates dissatisfied than a fool satisfied."

23. Though he spent much of his adult life seeking the acceptance and recognition of others, he argued that it's better for a ruler to be feared than loved.

24. He claimed that life without government is "solitary, poor, nasty, brutish, and short."

25. This 1930s slogan adapted from ads for DuPont is also the title of an album by Fatboy Slim.

26. This famous maxim, often wrongly attributed to Sir Francis Bacon, actually appears in a work by Thomas Hobbes from 1658.

27. This 1945 book gave us the slogan "All animals are equal but some are more equal than others."

28. The free market works like an invisible hand, according to a 1776 book by this Scottish philosopher.

29. "Nonsense on stilts" is the phrase applied by this English philosopher to the claim that there are inalienable natural rights.

30. He argued that we live in the best of all possible worlds, so Voltaire mocked him as Dr. Pangloss.

II

The *Jeopardy!* Moment

5
Dumberer and Smarterer

Timothy Sexton

One of the odder moments of the 2012 Republican Presidential nominating campaign featured former Pennsylvania Senator Rick Santorum receiving applause from a crowd of supporters after saying, "President Obama once said he wants everybody in America to go to college—what a snob!"

It may be hard to believe that such an old-fashioned suspicion of higher education as elitism still existed in 2012, but the evidence suggests that while Americans admire smart people, there still seems to be an ingrained mistrust of anyone who appears to be too smart. History has proved that Santorum is definitely not the only American who finds that a person revealed to be much smarter than the average Joe is likely to be either an elitist who wants to use that superior intelligence as a weapon of control . . . or a cheater.

The legacy of TV quiz shows that has led to millions of Americans becoming addicted to the nightly appearance of *Jeopardy!* on their local channel played a part in the latter suspicion. But that still doesn't explain why Santorum and so many others are so quick to view academic knowledge as some kind of boogey man. On the other hand, it may go a long way toward explaining the choice of Presidential candidates that usually gets past Iowa and New Hampshire.

I'll Take TV History for $500, Alex

September 13th, 1955. More than fifty million Americans are glued to their television sets as Richard McCutcheon stands on the verge of becoming the very first contestant to actually correctly answer the question that will reward him with $64,000, thus making the title of *The $64,000 Question* more than just a tease. What was that question? Name the five dishes and the two wines that were served by King George VI when he dined with Albert Lebrun, the President of France. Whew! Can you imagine Rick Santorum's reaction to *that* kind of snobby knowledge!

November 19th, 1999. Millions are glued to their TV sets to watch the hottest new show on TV, *Who Wants to Be a Millionaire?*, as John Carpenter is set to become the first contestant to actually answer the question that will net him a million bucks. What was that question? Which US President appeared on the TV series *Laugh-In*? Carpenter's quiz question was multiple choice: LBJ, Richard Nixon, Jimmy Carter, or Gerald Ford.

Has the quiz show been dumbed down since the 1950s or were people just smarter back then? Three contestants will attempt to answer that question later in this chapter. Before you leap to your own quick conclusion, you should know that, according to the District Attorney in charge of investigating the quiz show scandals of the 1950s, Richard McCutcheon admitted that he had been given a warm up drill prior to his first actual appearance on TV as a contestant on *The $64,000 Question*. He wasn't given the correct answers to any of the warm-up questions he missed, but full disclosure by one of those who were there during the infamous Quiz Show Scandals of the 1950s discloses that some of the questions he answered correctly in the privacy of the producer's office showed up again while he was on live TV.

On the other hand, Richard Nixon's rigid cameo on *Laugh-In* has become perhaps the most iconic moment in the collision between politics and television comedy shows. The fact that Nixon's awkward delivery of the show's catchphrase "Sock it to me!" has been repeated ad nauseam since it first occurred really makes an awareness of Nixon's appearance on the iconic 1960s variety show not that much different from a pre-show warm-up of the kind that McCutcheon received. It's always a question of when you learned the information demanded of you, rather than where or how you learned it.

What Is Hoodwinking?

Highly esoteric knowledge of the type that McCutcheon seemed to display was a regular part of the scandals of the 1950s, but it would be a mistake to assume that the contestants back then didn't actually possess that knowledge. If we're to take the words of the participants at face value, then the standard operating procedure was not to feed contestants with brand new information, but rather to find out what they already knew and then make sure questions asked on the show called for answers based on that knowledge. Public revelation of this facet of the scandal likely had something to do with *Jeopardy!* being designed to cover such a broad swath of knowledge over the breadth of its boards. Who could possibly know all that stuff beforehand and so quickly retrieve it from their memory at the touch of the buzzer—signaling device—allowing them to ring in?

If we assume that most winners of quiz shows aired during the quiz show's primetime heyday in the 1950s did actually know the answers to the questions that won them money, it would not be entirely unreasonable to suggest that, yes, the quiz show has been dumbed down in the intervening decades. But the story's more complicated than that. In fact, the state of game-show knowledge has gone through an ebb and flow resulting in fluctuations that paradoxically allow the answer to truthfully be yes, but with the caveat that the game show has also been smartened up since the scandal that brought down the genre. At least it has received its doctoral candidature in the form of one very popular entry that even legitimized betting as part of its appeal.

Jeopardy! exists as the offspring of the original philosophical architecture of the television quiz show. The foundation of that architectural design was based on a certain undeniable element of elitism. Those capable of answering questions such as those posed to McCutcheon were lifted to a level of knowledge far above the masses. While millions of viewers could probably have correctly answered Carpenter's million-dollar question, almost certainly a much smaller percentage of the viewing public could have correctly answered that $64,000 question. Toss in the added advantage of multiple choices, and the percentage of those capable of correctly deducing the correct answer of Richard Nixon increases significantly.

The Categories Are: Trivia, Religion, Ancient Civilizations, Games, Television and Feel-Good-Osophy

The appearance of *Jeopardy!* on television screens in the 1960s was like the discovery of Gnostic texts considered to have long been lost. Gnostic religious sects derive their name from the Greek word for knowledge: gnosis. Knowledge and quiz shows intertwined to a much more intimate degree than knowledge and other game shows, but within the generic world of television programming, *Jeopardy!* is no different than *The Price Is Right*. Philosophically, however, things are a bit different. And the comparison of *Jeopardy!* to the rediscovery of Gnostic philosophy is an apt one relative to the death of the original quiz-show concept as a result of the cheating scandals.

The unique rules and idiosyncratic structure of *Jeopardy!* as a game that sends contestants in search of the question rather than the answer must be viewed in philosophical terms as a reply to the fallout of the quiz show scandals of the 1950s. That public relations nightmare resulted in a fundamental and comprehensive transformation of the basic ideological intent of the TV game show.

Each of Our Contestants Today Was Educated Overseas

The quiz show scandals undermined the elitist stranglehold on knowledge. At the time, the educational philosophy of the American school system was undergoing an upheaval. The scandals may not have directly affected the upheaval, but they symbolically parallel it.

The personification of the profound psychological effect of that revelation could not have been more perfectly realized. Charles Van Doren was the son of a Pulitzer-Prize-winning author and on his way to a career as an Ivy League professor when he became the first reality-show celebrity by breaking the bank on the quiz show *Twenty-One*. Van Doren's success and popularity cemented him as the very idea of elitist knowledge come to life. The well-mannered, handsome Van Doren enjoyed a winning streak that quickly earned him $129,000— over a million in today's money. He had his picture on the cover of *Time* magazine, and his path was smoothed to prestigious broadcasting and writing jobs.

When allegations of quiz-show cheating began to grow, Van Doren at first flatly denied everything, but later admitted he had been supplied with questions and answers before the show. Even after his guilt became public knowledge, Van Doren was made editor of the *Encyclopaedia Britannica* and commissioned to write popular textbooks. The quiz-show scandal and Van Doren's part in it were enacted in the popular and controversial 1994 movie, *Quiz Show*.

In *Rules of the Game: Quiz Shows and American Culture* (2006), Olaf Hoerschelmann analyzes how the questions posed on the pre-scandal quiz shows reveal an elitist philosophy toward education and knowledge. Hoerschelmann suggests that during the Cold War there was a rising sense that a more utilitarian type knowledge was preferable to the somewhat exclusive model that looked to the classics and a higher level of knowledge.

According to Hoerschelmann, the type of progressive education that had reached its peak during the late 1930s and early 1940s was perceived as elitist by conservative critics. The progressive movement in America had moved further and further away from, and was even actually misconstruing, John Dewey's view of progressivism as a means of expanding a child's imagination, creativity, and openness to experience.

In *Left Back: A Century of Failed School Reforms* (2000), Diane Ravitch devotes an entire chapter to what she terms "The Great Meltdown" of the progressive movement in American education that first took root during the 1930s and continually gained momentum. The real impetus for change was the 1944 publication of a report titled *Education for All American Youth* by the Educational Policies Commission arm of the National Education Association. With the full consent and approval of the national organizations representing administrators and principals of public schools across the country, this report outlined a wholesale reform of the philosophy of education based on the progressive movement, taking it as far away as possible from any hint of elitism. Education needed to teach American kids how to arm themselves with the practical knowledge necessary to win the Cold War. This movement away from elitism to a more equalitarian approach is reflected in the shift from quiz show to game show.

For $300 in the Category "Before and After" . . . and You Have Found the Daily Double in Today's *Jeopardy!* Round

The death of the quiz show as a result of the scandals that transformed Charles Van Doren from the cover icon of *Time Magazine* into a semi-reclusive symbol of public shame had an immediate and intense effect on the very nature of the show itself. Those shows like *Twenty-One* and *The $64,000 Question* that demanded expert knowledge of the obscure, arcane, and abstruse, almost overnight turned into the non-elitist game shows of the 1960s highlighted by such blockbuster ratings successes as *The Dating Game, The Newlywed Game, Let's Make a Deal*, and *Match Game*. Knowledge-based shows still existed, but with a fundamental difference: success on these shows was now open to non-members of the intellectual elite since the focus was shifted from academic knowledge to more widely-shared everyday trivia. You could expect to take home a greater prize for knowing the cost of grocery products or determining if Paul Lynde was correctly answering a question or bluffing, or for being intensely aware of the slightest trivial quirk of your spouse, than for possessing knowledge such as which wines some powered-down British monarch served a President of France.

None of the quiz shows introduced in the early 1960s caught the public's attention like those earlier quiz shows that had shot like a meteor over the public's consciousness before the cheating scandal brought them crashing down to earth. The next generation of television quiz shows rarely lasted as long as something like *The Dating Game* or *Let's Make a Deal*. Quiz shows were replaced by "game shows." Whereas the word "quiz" has an inescapable tie to academia and a connotation just as likely to be negative as positive, the term "game" essentially does away with any negativity as well as exploding the fear that you must be a member of an elite to take part. Everybody plays games and most aren't graded on them.

The only quiz shows that remotely resembled those of the 1950s were things like *Quiz Bowl* and *Alumni Fun*. The very name of these shows indicated to prospective audiences that there was an elitist academic nature to them. What really separated these academic tournaments from the quiz shows of the past as well as the game shows against which they competed was not that they pitted teams of contestants against each other, but that the elitist quality of the participants was made concrete. *Quiz Bowl* is actually a parachute term that encompasses a vast line of televised quiz tournaments with names like *Academic Challenge, As Schools Match Wits, Scholastic Scrimmage*, and *It's Academic*. These shows were mostly local programming. The contestants were rarely viewed as individual heroes; they were viewed as a collective entity representing their scholastic institution. This is quite unlike the way in which the classic quiz show contestants were packaged, molded, and sold to viewers as everyday people with a grasp of academic knowledge.

The *Quiz Bowl* shows undermined admiration and superiority by implicitly imprinting the message that it took a *team* of brains to win while at the same time increasing the elitist chasm by constantly reminding viewers of the academic status of the contestants via the transmission provided by how largely the name of the school loomed.

W-o-l-f . . . um, . . . B-l-i-t-z-e-r

Most 1960s game shows veered away from the quiz show structure and introduced ways to win that relied far less on intellectual capacity than on the ability to gamble correctly or dress in the craziest manner or engage in nutty physical acts or reveal the most engaging personality. An even better way to win was by relying on the help of a celebrity. The game-show atmosphere of the immediate post-scandal period is the Dark Ages of the quiz show.

The admirable qualities of the pre-scandal shows and the genuine accomplishments of the majority of contestants who were not given answers beforehand were not just buried and forgotten. The memory and the positive qualities of those shows fell under a pall. Suddenly, the admiration for elitist intellectuals was gone and replaced by a curiously ironic elitism based on non-elitist ideals as well as the embrace of anti-intellectualism. The questions that animated the quiz shows of the 1950s were too obscure and rather than revealing the beauty of academic knowledge they had come to be seen more as a spit in the face of the common man.

Knowledge that aligned quite nicely with the more utilitarian philosophy of education sweeping the American school system proved far more useful on a typical post-scandal game show like *The Price Is Right*, where being of a class that knows the value of a can of soup is far more useful than being able to rattle off the names of the wives of Henry VIII and the manner in which each shuffled off her mortal coil.

The Price Is Right reflects the ideological shift in American education to the Right during the 1950s. If the quiz shows could be seen as the mainstream entertainment paradigm of the elitist philosophy of educational theory, and the scandal associated with them represents the symbolic death knell that masquerades its anti-academic bias under the pretense of a more democratic back-to-basics focus, then the game shows that replaced them during the 1960s are a perfectly aligned representative of that implicit suspicion of an intelligence that carries the stink of Santorum's view of snobbery.

Charles Van Doren, Herbert Stempel, and Richard McCutcheon possessed the kind of esoteric knowledge that is completely at odds with a sharply defined education system seeking in the words of Ravitch, to become "a custodial institution for the community's children, keeping them busy and preparing them for the existing social order."

It would be too simple to describe the undermining of the progressive educational movement as an attempt to "dumb down" the populace. But moving the aim away from more academic pursuits of less useful knowledge to a decidedly more utilitarian education designed with the specific overriding purpose of teaching kids how to become successful workers, producers, and consumers in order to keep the Communists at bay, is paralleled by a de-evolution in the quiz show format that can be described as "dumbed down."

The bias against the elitist leftovers in the progressive curriculum was actually framed in a way that determined it to be undemocratic in its focus on preparing an elite minority with the ability to pass their college entrance exams rather than preparing the much larger majority with the knowledge necessary to solve the problems of daily life—problems that had little if anything to do with any subject that turned a contestant on *Twenty-One* or *The $64,000 Question* into a much wealthier person overnight.

What Is—I Mean I'll Take Origins for $100

When it debuted in its original form in 1964, *Jeopardy!* contrasted with the herd of other game shows by its return to the more sophisticated, elitist style of the pre-scandal quiz shows. What really made *Jeopardy!* stand out from the pack, however, was its most singular innovation: instead of providing an answer to a question, contestants had to provide a question to the answer.

As well as forcing contestants to provide the "answer" in a strictly regimented formulated response, the show ended with the requirement that contestants actually write down that answer while still abiding by those rules of phrasing. What really separates *Jeopardy!* from all of its competitors is its finely nuanced balance between elitism and non-elitism: it steers clear of the more arcane intellectual knowledge that viewers might have assumed was more evidence of cheating, while also managing to require a very strong element of the elitist knowledge that was a hallmark of the scandals. The return of *Jeopardy!* in syndicated format in the 1980s really cemented its status as the archetypal compromise between the elitist and anti-elitist models for TV game shows.

Jeopardy! established its position as the Gnostic gospel of lost ancient knowledge discovered in a desert of low-level celebrities sitting inside a giant tic-tac-toe grid, grown men dressed in horse costumes looking to make a deal, and contestants putting their egalitarian education to the test by guessing the price of a brand new car. The height of these alternative games peaked in the 1970s.

The central philosophical doctrine of Gnosticism is based on the collapse of integration between the divine and the mortal as a result of some catastrophic separation. Man and God originally belonged together, which fits nicely with the idea of an elitist struggle for attainment of a knowledge that is "higher" than that which merely facilitates a base existence. It is the sphere of the worldly that is situated as the object of division between man and God reintegrating.

With the exception of the more sharply defined academic interest of the Quiz Bowls, *Jeopardy!* faced little in the way of competition from similar programming. It would not be until the dawn of the twenty-first century that this situation would change and the result would serve only to heighten the show's unique position as the ultimate hybrid of quiz and game shows as well as the most Gnostic of all attempts to unite the genre with its godlike past—without the cheating, this time.

Who Is Brad Pitt the Elder?

A *Washington Post* article published at the height of the second-generation prime time quiz show craze says it all in its title: "Are Questions on Latest Batch of Quiz Shows Easier or What?"

Paul Farhi's article notes that the *Jeopardy!* challenger which has so far come closest to knocking it off its perch as America's Quiz Show, *Who Wants to Be a Millionaire?*, contained questions offering dollar amounts that dwarfed significantly more difficult *Jeopardy!* Queries, demanding such knowledge as the year Columbus discovered America and the state in which you can find the Empire State Building.

Iconic quiz-show scandal figure Herbert Stempel provides the most incisive observation of the many who chime in on the obvious dumbing down of questions on game shows by noting that what passes for arcane knowledge on esoteric subjects today is nothing less than an insult to those who honestly answered the types of questions posed on the shows that made up the original prime time quiz craze.

Sociologist Todd Gitlin suggests that the body politic of American society changed during the period from *The $64,000 Question* to *Who Wants to Be a Millionare?* This change is manifested in the form of a viewing public that once enjoyed being stumped because they took it as a sign that they could always learn something new to a public more eager to display knowledge already collected. The new generation of quiz shows differ substantially from *Jeopardy!* by being popular because most viewers can correctly answer more of the questions correctly. Often, in fact, the draw seems to be based on a feeling of superiority over contestants who are far more subject to derision for not knowing an answer generally perceived as "obvious" than any contestant on the pre-scandal shows.

Former Richard Nixon speechwriter and titular game show host Ben Stein boils things down much more bluntly and, perhaps, most truthfully with his self-deprecating but discerning admission that the level of intellectual acquisition in America has reached such a low level that he might well be considered the early twenty-first-century equivalent of a Charles Van Doren, Herbert Stempel, or Richard McCutcheon—or perhaps better stated, as one of those original quiz show contestants whose exceptional intelligence so admired by viewers tuning in religiously every week was not corrupted by the stain of deceit.

Today's Final Clue in the Category of Discarded TV Show Titles Is "What's the Question?"

Jeopardy! introduced a more trivial aspect of knowledge to quiz shows, but managed to retain the authoritarian and elitist principles of the format by proposing that the possession of knowledge is not enough: you must also display that knowledge in a ritualistic manner by phrasing the answer in the form of a question. Putting forth questions is a distinctly Socratic methodology of trading in philosophic wisdom that allows *Jeopardy!* to rise above its proletarian grasp of trivial knowledge so that it seems as if the contestants possess a greater wisdom than they actually might. This concept reaches its apotheosis with Final Jeopardy!, which requires the WRITTEN WORD that is PROPERLY PHRASED (and even sometimes properly spelled) in order to win.

6
Jeopardy! Monkeys Ain't Smart

Robert Arp

If I heard it once, I must've heard it a thousand times growing up: "Those contestants on *Jeopardy!* sure are smart. They know *so* much!" I used to believe it, too, until I came to realize that they just have a really good ability to recall facts through what psychologists and other researchers call *declarative memory*.

For years now, we've been able to get monkeys to memorize all kinds of information and recall it on command by pressing levers, bars, and even buzzers just like *Jeopardy!* contestants. The famous anthropologist, Kathleen Gibson, speaks of a captive monkey named Andy who was able to associate written words with pictures on flashcards, as well as spoken words with numerous objects and items in his home and neighborhood. Penny Patterson and other ape researchers have been able to get gorillas like the famous Koko, chimps like Kanzi, and orangutans like Chantek to learn sign language, and answer basic questions like, "What is the capital of the United States?" "What letter comes after B?" and "How many fingers am I holding up?" Being smart or knowledgeable isn't merely about memorizing and recalling facts on command—it's more about explaining and synthesizing facts, as well as using facts in analysis and critique through argumentation.

Bloomin' Bloom!

There's a model of learning objectives that's been around for years now (especially in the US education system), called *Bloom's Taxonomy*, named after American educator, Benjamin

Bloom (1913–1999). Since its introduction in the 1950s, the Taxonomy has changed a bit and has been adapted by numerous researchers and teachers in a variety of ways, but the basic objectives are presented in Table 1.

TABLE 1: Bloom's Taxonomy

OBJECTIVE / LEVEL NAME	WHAT THE STUDENT SHOULD ACCOMPLISH
KNOWLEDGE	Recall, reproduce, recognize, list, define, name, and/or outline data, facts, or information
COMPREHENSION	Understand the meaning of, as well as explain, paraphrase, summarize, and/or distinguish various types of data, facts, or information
APPLICATION	Utilize, change, manipulate, and/or modify data, facts, or information in relation to some problem to be solved, as well as give evidence and examples of data, facts, or information
ANALYSIS	Separate, differentiate, deconstruct, and/or break down data, facts, or information into basic components or parts so that the foundational structure may be understood
SYNTHESIS	Build, combine, compile, construct, and/or generalize about data, facts, or information, with an emphasis on creating a new meaning or structure
EVALUATION	Critique, judge, justify, and/or appraise data, facts, or information, as well as show implications, entailments, and/or consequences related to data, facts, or information

These objectives can be used in elementary, high school, and college classrooms, and not only have I had them used on me when I was a student in college, but I've also utilized them as a benchmark for grading in the high school religion and college philosophy and world religion courses I have taught over the years.

    The overall goal of the Taxonomy is to identify capabilities that students will acquire as they learn and proceed from one level to the next, which is really the same thing as becoming smart or knowledgeable about some topic or area of study. However, notice that there's a kind of easier-to-harder progression that goes from basic KNOWLEDGE through to EVALUATION (top to bottom, in the table). In fact, it's probably the case that the standard D student can barely accomplish the KNOWLEDGE level, while your A students in class likely can achieve SYNTHESIS and EVALUATION. That's the way I used the Taxonomy in my own grading of students in religion and philosophy courses. The smart or knowledgeable students were the ones who didn't just define, name, or list ideas and concepts; they were able to construct and compile, critique and criticize, as well as judge and justify, data, facts, information, ideas, concepts, and arguments.

Now, here's something interesting to note: in some later versions of the Taxonomy, the KNOWLEDGE level is actually renamed REMEMBERING or RECALLING. This is probably because what people do at this level isn't knowledge, really. It's just spitting back what data, facts, or information you have stored in your memory banks. *Jeopardy!* contestants are great at recalling, reproducing, listing, and naming data, facts, or information. Again, so are monkeys, as well as chimps, gorillas, and orangutans. If I had a *Jeopardy!* contestant in one of my classes, and all the person did was what they do on *Jeopardy!* by simply recalling and remembering things, then she or he would likely barely pass the class.

Remembering that Memory Is Still Important

So, what I'm suggesting so far is that real smarts or knowledge occurs more toward the EVALUATION end of Bloom's Taxonomy. This isn't to say that memory and reproducing facts aren't valuable to knowledge. Of course they are, since you have to be able to recall facts in the process of analyzing, synthesizing, or evaluating, and the more evaluating you do, the more memory and recollection you seem to require.

John Locke (1632–1704) popularized the idea that the mind is an immense *tabula rasa*—a blank slate—and numerous psychologists, neuroscientists, philosophers, and other thinkers since Locke have demonstrated that a person can "write" countless ideas on the mind throughout a lifetime, in terms of storing memories. Also, it goes without saying that when we read the writings of those we consider to be the smartest, most knowledgeable people in human history—for example, Aristotle, Confucius, St. Thomas Aquinas, Sir Isaac Newton, or Albert Einstein—it's likely that they acquired an almost encyclopedic memory of the things they wrote about. Further, listen to or read the words of any person you consider smart who's living today—like Stephen Hawking, Peter Singer, or members of Mensa International—and you'll see that they have an incredible amount of stored information in their own memory banks.

Belee Dat!

Being smart is also thought of as being knowledgeable, and they're probably interchangeable terms in many ways. So, the real question we're in interested in is: What is knowledge? This is a question that epistemologists explore. *Epistemology* is the branch of philosophy concerned with the source and nature of knowledge (*episteme* is Greek for "knowledge") as well as what constitutes the truth, evidence, and justification of our beliefs or opinions. There's an idea that goes all the way back to Plato's dialogue, *Theaetetus*, that knowledge consists of 1. a *belief* that is 2. *true* and 3. *justified*. Ever since then, philosophers have been debating mostly about what truth and justification mean.

The belief part is pretty easy to understand. Humans can reason, and no one disputes that. What enables them to reason, most people call a *mind*, which *is* a disputed thing since there are those who think that the "mind" is an illusion, and all that really is taking place when people reason is, at best, a series of brain processes and functions. Putting this debate aside, everyone who reasons admits that they form beliefs, opinions, and thoughts about themselves, the world, and reality as they perceive it. So, knowledge includes believing something: to know is to, at least, *believe* something is the case. When you're watching *Jeopardy!*, and the answer is "He was the first philosopher in the history of Western philosophy," and you scream at the TV, "I know the question to this one!" you at least *believe*, have the *opinion*, or form the *thought* that it's "Who is Thales of Miletus?"

It Just Has to Be True . . . I Know It

But believing, having an opinion about, or merely forming a thought about something isn't enough to know something. One of my students in a philosophy of biology class claimed this: "Humans evolved from monkeys—this I know for sure." But I didn't really think he *knew* that. Why? Because it's just not true. Monkeys and humans evolved from a common ancestral prosimian. In fact, a whole bunch of people on the planet— believe it or not—think that humans evolved *from* monkeys! And, a whole bunch of people on the planet *know* nothing about the truth concerning simian evolution, unfortunately.

Numerous times during a *Jeopardy!* show someone will believe or think they have the correct question and press the signal button, only to find out after they provide their question that it's incorrect. They may even say to themselves in an instant, "Oooh! I *know* this one!," but because the question they offer to Alex Trebek is incorrect, they really don't "*know* this one."

So, knowledge includes a belief, opinion, or thought about something, but the belief, opinion, or thought also has to be *true*. No one is said to be knowledgeable when all of what they believe is false. The people who win on *Jeopardy!* know a lot of stuff that is true (that is, when they actually do know the questions, and aren't merely guessing); the losers usually don't know as many *true* answers. Hard-core creationists, Ku Klux Klansmen, members of the Flat Earth Society, Holocaust deniers, and Moon-landing deniers all have something in common, too: they're all know-nothing idiots. They have their crazy beliefs, but their beliefs are just that—crazy and untrue!

Now, there's a lot of debate about what truth is, or whether it even exists. The most common-sense view of truth is known as the *correspondence theory of truth*. According to this theory, if a belief that someone has actually corresponds to or matches up with some state of affairs in the world or in reality, then the belief is true. If the belief doesn't correspond, it's false. This makes sense to most of us who think that there's a distinction between a. our *beliefs about* the world or reality and b. the world or reality *as it really is*. Notice that we can have beliefs, opinions, or thoughts about the world that are just plain wrong or false— like with our creationist or Moon-landing denier friends—and they're false because they don't correspond with reality.

Alex Trebek, the folks who put together the questions at *Jeopardy!*, the contestants, and we the viewers all assume the correspondence theory of truth is . . . well . . . true. A true or correct question given by a contestant is one that matches up or corresponds with the actual "answer" provided by Alex; a false or incorrect question given by a contestant is one that doesn't match up or correspond with the answer.

Truth by Accident

It's still not enough for knowledge to say that you have true beliefs. This is going to sound strange, but it could be the case that you have a true belief about something, yet, you don't *know* that something. You could have a true belief by accident, for example, which is a point that Plato made more than two thousand years ago in the *Theaetetus*.

Let's say you thought my first name was Ron, instead of Rob, and someone asked you if you knew my name and what the first letter of my name was. You then said, "Yeah, I know that guy, and I know his name, and it begins with an R." This would be a true belief because my name does begin with an R; but because you thought my name was Ron, instead of Rob, you could not accurately be said to *know* my name, despite having the true belief about my name starting with an R.

I actually know a guy who was on *Jeopardy!* in 1988, and he won the first day by answering the following "answer" in the Final *Jeopardy!* Round: "The typical wasp uses this material to construct its nest." He told me that he really didn't know the answer (the question) at all, but made an educated guess. While the "ding, ding, ding, ding . . ." theme we all know so well was playing, he looked up into the air and thought about the fact that a wasp nest looks kind of like parchment paper. So he wrote down, "What is tree pulp?" It turns out he was lucky, and was the only one of the three who guessed correctly. Again, he didn't *know* the question, really, and many contestants make educated guesses in the Final Jeopardy! Round and end up winning because of it. Also, it's probably the case that monkeys and apes do a bit of educated guessing on association tests, showing that they really don't know the answer either, as psychologists will admit in studies.

The older guy who was on *Jeopardy!* in 1988 wagered a fairly conservative one thousand dollars, by the way, and he lost the next day "to some know-it-all cocky bastard in a three-piece suit who barely shook my hand." It's funny how these folks with good memories, or who are good guessers, who aren't really so smart *think* they're really so smart.

Justify It

Most importantly, when someone claims they know something, we want to know the reason why they know that something. In other words, we want some kind of *justification* for what they claim to know. Remember from Plato that we said knowledge consists of 1. a *belief* that is 2. *true* and 3. *justified*? "What's your justification for the belief that you think is true?" is a common, explicit (or implicit) question that anyone who's doing serious thinking asks, whether it's in a philosophy classroom, during a presidential debate, through the course of a civil trial, or in an interview with a scientist about her latest hypothesis.

Although what exactly is meant by it has been a controversial topic since Plato, justification usually begins with an explanation that includes evidence. Recall also that in Bloom's Taxonomy, COMPREHENSION and APPLICATION are the levels usually achieved after KNOWLEDGE/ REMEMBERING/ RECALLING. If you look at the descriptions of COMPREHENSION and APPLICATION, you'll see that COMPREHENSION includes being able to explain something, while APPLICATION includes being able to provide evidence and examples of something. In fact, Plato's student, Aristotle (384–322 B.C.E.), made a big deal about knowledge consisting of explanation and evidence, and if you read any of his works, you'll see that he walks his own talk. Aristotle was not only a philosopher, he was also one of the first scientists, and scientists are usually looked at today as *the* smart or knowledgeable people on the planet—especially rocket scientists, right?—mostly because they can explain and provide evidence and examples for their hypotheses, ideas, concepts, and arguments.

But, as I've hinted at already, I would argue that ANALYSIS, SYNTHESIS, and EVALUATION are the hallmarks of justification, probably with EVALUATION being the most important. If you believe that your data, facts, information, ideas, or concepts are true and can break them down into fundamental explanatory parts (ANALYSIS), or can construct something coherent and systematic with them (SYNTHESIS), then you're well on your way to knowledge about them. Further, if you can also critique and appraise your data, facts, information and the like, as well as show implications, entailments, and/or consequences related to them (EVALUATION), then you *really* know your stuff!

This is what philosophers do, so that's why we're usually the smartest, most knowledgeable people on the planet J. I say *usually* because some of us ain't the sharpest tools in the shed, if you know what I mean. (I would put myself in the dull category, so as to offend equally and to equally offend.) In any event, I always try to justify my true beliefs—and I have required the same from my students and others who put forward positions—through achieving Bloom's EVALUATION level, which just so happens to be the level of *real* smarts or knowledge.

Arguing . . . in a Good Way

More can be said about the EVALUATION level of Bloom's Taxonomy, which happens to coincide with being a smarty pants. In my philosophy classes, I always made the students put forward arguments for their beliefs, opinions, and thoughts, and I always made them critique the arguments of others.

You can offer an argument as a form of justification, too. An *argument* is a set of claims, one of which is known as the *conclusion*, which is supposed to be supported, demonstrated, or shown to be the case by another claim (or claims) known as a *premise*. A *claim* is a statement, proposition, or declarative sentence that is either true or false, and is the result of a belief, opinion, or thought you have about yourself, the world, or reality as you perceive it.

An argument is used to show that the conclusion put forward either: 1. is supported by a premise (or premises) and is *absolutely true* in what is known as a *deductive argument*; or 2. is supported by a premise (or premises) and is *likely or probably true* in what is known as an *inductive argument*. Now, whether you succeed in demonstrating the absolute or likely truth of your conclusion is another matter, since you can *think* that your conclusion follows from a premise or premises, when it in fact doesn't (here, you'd have what is known as a *fallacy*), or your premises may be false, in which case your conclusion will be either absolutely false (in a deductive argument), likely false (in an inductive argument), or simply unsupported.

When all's said and done, then, people who can put forward good arguments for their beliefs, opinions, concepts, and the like are the smartest, most knowledge people. Again, this is what us philosophers do J. Here's my argument for arguments being a mark of smarts:

> **Premise 1:** You are really, truly smart/knowledgeable about your data, facts, information and the like *if and only if* you can meaningfully critique and appraise them, as well as show implications, entailments, and/or consequences related to them (EVALUATION) *by putting forward good arguments*.

> **Premise 2:** That philosopher critiqued and appraised the data . . . by putting forward a good argument.

> ---

> **Conclusion:** That philosopher really, truly is smart or knowledgeable.

Note also this argument and conclusion:

> **Premise 1:** You are really, truly smart or knowledgeable about your data, facts, information and the like *if and only if* you can meaningfully critique and appraise them, as well as show implications, entailments, or consequences related to them (EVALUATION) *by putting forward good arguments*.

> **Premise 2:** *Jeopardy!* contestants don't critique and appraise data . . . by putting forward good arguments.

> ---

> **Conclusion:** *Jeopardy!* contestants ain't smart.

Jumping to Conclusions and . . . the Conclusion, Too

Smart people generally try not to draw conclusions that are not supported by the premises they are using. When you do make the mistake of drawing a conclusion that is unsupported by the premises being used, the technical name for that bad bit of reasoning is "committing a *fallacy*." A common way to say this is that you've jumped to a conclusion. If Frank thinks, "they're all gonna be lemons like that" based upon a few instances or examples of that kind of car being a lemon, then he's jumped to a conclusion incorrectly. Frank really doesn't have any grounds for thinking that *all* of the future cars of that kind are necessarily gonna be lemons. Or, you're jumping to a conclusion if you think, "This guy's gonna definitely win on *Jeopardy!*" *because* he's a philosopher, or even *because* he's a rocket scientist (since they're *all* so smart, right?).

Now, I have to be careful not to jump to the conclusion that all contestants on *Jeopardy!* aren't smart, and let me explain what I mean, especially since I've been making the case all along in this chapter that they ain't smart. It's incorrect to think that smarts *is equated with* recalling information only, as if there's nothing else to smarts. That's actually the way I used to think about the smarts of *Jeopardy!* contestants when I was younger, and it's incorrect.

However, it's likely that a lot of the folks on *Jeopardy!* not only have great declarative memories that they display (like good monkeys) on the show, but they also likely can do the analysis, synthesis, and evaluation stuff—including putting forward good arguments—that *is* necessary for smarts. I wouldn't *jump* to the conclusion that *Jeopardy!* contestants are or aren't smart, actually, but I would wager that it's probably the case that a lot of them are smart. No fallacy in thinking this.

That old guy who was on *Jeopardy!* in 1988 actually is a trained philosopher, so although he wasn't really displaying smarts as a contestant, he often displays smarts in the evaluation and arguing he does regularly in the classroom and on paper with books and articles he writes. He even told me this one time, which was actually the catalyst for my wanting to write this chapter in the first place:

> People have said to me, 'You must be smart . . . you were on *Jeopardy!*', but I tell them that I'm a lucky guesser *and* I'm lucky to have been blessed with a really good memory.

7

I, for One, Welcome Our New Computer Overlords

NICOLAS MICHAUD

Ken Jennings and Brad Rutter are smart men. They are *very* smart men. Jennings won seventy-four games of *Jeopardy!* in a row, and Rutter has won $3.2 million in *Jeopardy!* earnings. And, so, I am comfortable admitting they are both a good deal smarter than me, in fact.

It's not easy to beat them when it comes to being smart, if being smart is evidenced by winning at *Jeopardy!,* but there is one "individual" that made beating Jennings and Rutter seem relatively easy: Both men simultaneously suffered a relatively crushing defeat at the "hands" of Watson, an IBM-built "intelligent" machine. Jennings and his archrival Rutter were, well, spanked, by IBM's digital *Jeopardy!* juggernaut.

Don't get me wrong: Jennings and Rutter made a damn good show of it, even ending one game with a tie and passing Watson in earnings midst another, but the final score—$77,147 to $24,000 to $21,000, Watson to Jennings to Rutter—doesn't allow for much doubt. Watson won, soundly. But what does Watson's winning *mean*? Should we simply treat this event as a fluke, or admit that computers are better at answering questions than we are; or should we, as Jennings joked, quoting the *Simpsons,* "welcome our new computer overlords"?

The fact is that the computers are coming. Heck, they're already here. They have control of our credit histories, our banks, our knowledge stores like *Wikipedia,* and our nukes. Scientists around the world are competing to create robots who learn the way children do, computers who exhibit emotions, and robotic chairs that put themselves back together if taken apart. "Drone" aircraft are beginning to fight our wars, and in my lifetime we'll see robotic hands regularly performing surgery. Is Watson evidence of a step toward intelligent machines, or are they already here? If Watson is intelligent, how should we treat "him"? How should we treat this product of our genius? Intelligent machines are here, and getting smarter; if they beat us at chess and *Jeopardy!*, what will they beat us at next?

Would You Like to Play a Game?

The fact that Watson won a game of *Jeopardy!*, nonetheless against the most powerful human players who have ever played the game, is pretty significant in the worlds of philosophy and artificial intelligence. Philosophers have been arguing for a very long time about whether machines can or could think. One philosopher, Alan Turing (1912–1954), developed what he believed to be a very fair test of machine intelligence. He thought that a game, not unlike *Jeopardy!*, would be an excellent way to check for *thinking*. But not all philosophers agree that his test demonstrates that a machine is thinking, as opposed to acting as a very, *very*, complex abacus.

Let's consider Turing's idea. Turing was alive during World War II and was a British hero, working as a code-breaker for the Allies. His work in mathematics and machine intelligence was cut short when Turing killed himself. Ironically, as a man who advocated for the fair treatment of all intelligence, the government that he had helped win the "Great War" forced him to take hormonal treatments because he was homosexual; those treatments left him disfigured and in terrible pain, and so he took his life. Turing's legacy, though, is substantial.

Turing did groundbreaking work demonstrating how machines could display the ability to answer questions intelligently. For these reasons and for his work in mathematics he's considered one of the founders of modern computer theory. What's really amazing, though, is the fact that after he took those first ingenious and creative theoretical and mathematical steps, he went on to ask a ground-breaking question, "How would we know that a machine is intelligent?," and generate a legitimate philosophical test for that intelligence.

Turing's idea was, in essence, this: Imagine that you were on a game show like *Jeopardy!*. This exciting new game show is called . . . *Man or Machine?* The game only requires that you guess correctly whether the entity answering a set of questions is a machine or a human. In order to prevent contestants from answering the question based on the sound of the entity's voice or based on physical appearance, the contestant is only allowed to communicate with the answer via instant messaging or texting.

Imagine that you're called onto the stage, and Alex Trebek points to a mysterious door. He tells you that there is either a machine or a human behind the door, and that it will answer your questions via instant messaging. He gives you an hour to hold a conversation with whatever it is in the closet, and your goal is to figure out if it is a machine or a man. So you walk behind the keyboard on the stage and begin typing. Many might assume that if the entity that answers your questions is a human, then it possesses some degree of intelligence. What would you look for in order to determine if it is actually a machine?

Well, imagine that you hold a conversation with whatever is behind the door, and after an hour you decide that it must be a human behind the door. Alex asks you, "Why do you think it's a human in the closet?" You explain that the conversation was just too intelligent and too sensible to have been generated by a computer. Too much *understanding* was demonstrated by the answers to your questions, so, given the intelligent answers, you believe it must be a human. Alex opens the closet and BOOM! it is Watson, who says, now out loud, "Hi!" Many might respond, "Wow! I *thought* it was intelligent; now I feel foolish!" But how fair is that response?

Turing's point is that you believed what was behind the door was intelligent *until you found out it was Watson, a machine*. But that isn't very fair at all! You were so sure that the mystery answerer was intelligent that you assumed it was in fact human! But, how do you know that other humans are intelligent? The simple fact that something is human doesn't mean that it's intelligent. Corpses, for example, are human, but not intelligent. Given that you can't actually get into any other human's head, how do you know intelligent thought is going on behind their eyes?

We know someone else is intelligent when they respond to us in ways that demonstrate understanding. You believe that I am intelligent as opposed to a corpse or an automaton because when you speak with me, I answer your questions in a way that demonstrates understanding of your questions. But in our imaginary game, isn't that exactly what Watson did? Turing argues that if the machine can fool us, then we should be prudent, and assume it can function in an intelligent manner. We should assume that the machine is intelligent in the same way that we assume that a human is intelligent because of the way that he or she converses with us.

If we refuse to agree that Watson is intelligent in our imaginary scenario, we're doing so only because "he" is a machine. In other words, had you had the same exact instant messaging conversation with a human, you would say he or she was an intelligent, thinking, thing. So, when the door opens, and we see that it's actually Watson who has had this lengthy and insightful conversation with us, the only reason why we would change our minds is because it turned out to be a machine behind the door. And that doesn't seem fair at all. After all, we human beings are very complex machines, and we can think, so why couldn't another kind of machine also think?

No. What is 'Goofy Mistakes Only a Machine Could Make'?

The real Watson, the one who won in *Jeopardy!*, does something profound for proponents of Turing's philosophy. Watson, although never placed behind a door, was able to answer questions that were not even asked in question form. Think about how many human beings have difficulty understanding *Jeopardy!'s* Answer-to-Question format, and then realize that Watson, a machine, was able to navigate answering those questions with surprising ability.

The immediate response that many people have to the idea that Watson can actually think is to note the fact that he got some answers wrong, in a pretty silly way. For example, in the Final Jeopardy! question the clue was, "Its largest airport is named for a World War II hero; its second largest for a World War II battle." The audience couldn't help but laugh when Watson answered "What is Toronto?????" Perhaps even more problematically, Watson responded to the clue, "The first modern crossword puzzle is published and Oreo cookies are introduced" with the exact same *wrong* response Jennings had given only moments before, "The 1920s." How can we argue that Watson thinks when he makes such goofy mistakes and cannot learn from the mistakes of others?

Well, let's be fair. Watson can't hear. He had no idea what Jennings's wrong answer was. This in no way reflects on his intelligence, or capacity for intelligence, any more than it would for a human who could not hear. As for the Final Jeopardy! question, well, one might note that Watson is pretty young. How often do children make similar mistakes? I recall a friend of mine who chastised her father for drinking a soda while driving his truck because, "You aren't supposed to drink and drive, Daddy!" When a child makes a mistake like this, it isn't because they aren't thinking; it's because they don't have enough contextual knowledge to act in a way that demonstrates they understand the idea at hand. I don't think anyone would argue that my friend's chastisement of her father would mean that she isn't intelligent. She just made a mistake because of a lack of knowledge about the context.

The fact that Watson made mistakes may be no different from the way we all make mistakes in understanding when text messaging or instant messaging. We often need clarification because we misread or misinterpret a message that lacks context. Should we extend to Watson the same leniency that we extend to a child or a friend who misunderstands our texts? Mistakes in interpretation because of lack of contextual knowledge shouldn't be deemed evidence of lack of thought. They may indicate lack of understanding *of the context*, but not of the language.

Watson has never eaten a cookie: he lacks the experience of tasting one, holding one, or any other physical interaction with one. So, for him, the distinction between an Oreo cookie and an internet cookie found in a browser cache is not nearly as profound and tactile. This doesn't mean he doesn't think. We would make a similar mistake on a question that was similarly foreign to us. Imagine talking to a person who affirms a radically different religion or lives in a country with a drastically different system of government. You would ask many questions that may seem silly to that person, and you would likely make what seem to be silly mistakes. For example, imagine the surprise of Native Americans who were told by Catholic missionaries that they must eat and drink the blood of Christ—to the natives, it sounded like the missionaries were preaching cannibalism! Without the context and the experience, they did not understand what the missionaries were talking about.

I'll Take 'Baloney' for $200, Alex

A very famous living philosopher would take a great deal of objection to what I have argued here. John Searle has made much of his philosophical career finding flaws in Turing's arguments. Searle argues that passing the test Turing suggests doesn't necessarily mean any intelligence has been exhibited at all. He thinks that machines like Watson don't really understand words like "cookie." They just know the rules for applying "cookie," and therefore often get it wrong. From Searle's perspective, we might say that machines lack understanding— not just of general context, but the context necessary to understand what language is actually *about* at all. So, when Watson answered those questions on *Jeopardy!*, he was just, in essence, linking answers to questions, but without ever really understanding them.

It can be difficult to imagine how someone could answer questions without understanding them, which explains why Turing's argument is so powerful. But Searle asks us to rethink Turing's imaginary game. Recall that in our fictional game show, *Man or Machine?*, we ask a series of questions to whatever is behind the door, and if what's behind the door answers the questions and can converse with us like an intelligent agent, then we should treat it as such. If it happens to be a machine behind the door and we choose not to treat it like it is an intelligent thing, we're saying that the machine can't think *because it is a machine*. But if we are going to say that machines can't think, we need to know why. Searle thinks it is because they lack understanding, and he thinks he can show how our game show, and *Jeopardy!*, can be won by a machine that doesn't really understand the questions.

Searle asks us to imagine a game similar to Turing's. Imagine that you are going to compete on *Jeopardy!*, but instead of standing behind a podium, you are placed in a small room. You are supposed to provide the question for the clues, but here's the kicker. . . . Alex passes the clues to you written in a language you cannot read—let's imagine it is Chinese. So the question is messaged to you. But inside the "Chinese room" with you, you have a huge book with a bunch of English letters and Chinese characters called "The Big Book of Rules." The book provides no definitions. It only tells you that when you see one character, you write a specifically Chinese character. The book is basically a detailed set of directions for changing one symbol, or set of symbols, into another. So, you painstakingly look up every symbol of the clue that Alex passes to you and type in the corresponding Chinese character as the book instructs. When you finish, you send your reply back to Alex, and even though you don't understand Chinese, you were able to answer the question sensibly because you followed the rules the book gave you. Alex is able to read and understand your answer, and tells you that it is correct. As a result, everyone in the audience thinks you *understand* Chinese, when in fact you don't. You merely were able to move symbols around and draw one symbol when you saw another. Isn't that what computers like Watson do? They answer by following rules, but they don't understand the language; they just translate symbols as they are instructed.

So, from Searle's argument, it seems possible that someone, or something, could answer a series of questions, and *appear* to understand those questions, while, in reality, all that is happening is the person or machine (such as Watson), is just moving symbols around as per a set of instructions, or "code." Granted, if a human were acting as the machine as Searle has us imagine, it would take a very long time to create each answer due to having to look up directions for translating symbols. But Searle's point is that computers do exactly that, except super-fast.

Daily Double: Turing versus Searle

There are a couple of obvious questions that Searle's argument brings to mind. One is the fact that Turing's test requires that the machine and the man hold a lengthy, sensible conversation. If you were able to translate symbols in the Chinese room with that kind of fluidity, so that a robust conversation could be held, you sure as heck would seem to understand Chinese. Maybe it's true that *you* don't understand Chinese, but you, in combination with the Big Book of Rules, would create a system that does. Recall that we aren't talking about one question or even ten, but at least an hour's worth of engaged questioning and answering. So, there's good reason to think that you, in the case of the Chinese Room, are acting as a kind of a processor for a bigger thinking thing, a system that combines you and the book. You don't understand Chinese any more so than an Intel processor in a computer does, but the combination of you plus the book is able to hold a conversation that seems pretty demonstrative of understanding.

There's no way to prove that *anything* but you is a thinking thing. And that was Turing's most powerful point. You can never get into anyone's head, and you can never get into any computer's "head." Watson may just be translating symbols, or he may be taking the first steps towards understanding language. We can't be sure. All Turing asks us to do is extend the same courtesy to machines as we do to humans—if a machine converses like a thinking thing, then let's extend it the benefit of the doubt that it is a thinking thing. Wouldn't it be far worse to assume that something isn't a thinking thing, when it really is, than to assume the opposite?

Searle, on the other hand, does not want us to extend the benefit of the doubt. His arguments suggest not that we should not be careful about denying intelligence, but that we should be careful about assuming intelligence. But it's hard to see what harm can come from assuming something is a thinking thing and intelligent. His standard for membership in the club of "thinking things" seems so hard to achieve that the other major problem with Searle's argument is that no philosopher has been able to come up with a way for *anyone* to demonstrate the high-level of understanding Searle demands. Machines like Watson seem to be able to answer questions in numerous ways, and discriminate between answers that are more or less likely to be correct. In fact, Watson was designed to hesitate if he wasn't sufficiently sure that he had the right answer. What else can we ask of someone in terms of demonstrating that they understand a word?

Imagine that someone asks you to show that you understand the word "*Jeopardy!*", so you provide a definition. "Sure,

I know what *Jeopardy!* is! It is a game show in which the contestants are very smart and they compete to answer clues by providing the question." And your friend says she's still not convinced you understand what *Jeopardy!* is; after all, like in the Chinese room, you might just be providing a pre-programed definition you have memorized.

And so you give many connotations of *Jeopardy!*: you explain that it's a game, and that there are lots of kinds of games, some that are dissimilar to *Jeopardy!*, like football, and some that are kind of similar, like *Are You Smarter Than a 5th Grader?*. You explain that the host of *Jeopardy!* is Alex Trebek and that you're glad he grew his mustache back. Your friend, though, is still unsure: after all, you might just have been told to say all of those things, without ever knowing what they mean, like Watson being programmed; so, you turn on your TV and point to an episode of *Jeopardy!* And then you change the channel to a movie and you say, "This is the movie *Terminator*, not *Jeopardy!*" and then you change it back to *Jeopardy!* and say, "And this is still *Jeopardy!*" After that, what else could you do to prove you understand what Jeopardy is? You've given a strict definition, you've given many different connotations and associations, and you've even pointed out cases of *Jeopardy!* and not-*Jeopardy!*

Why, then, does Searle seem to want more from a machine? Watson seems like he could do many of the things listed above to demonstrate understanding. Some machines can even point at objects they haven't seen before and identify them. I recently saw a video of a computer program at E3 that was speaking with a programmer. The program was connected through an Xbox 360 Kinect, so it was able to see things. The program, whose avatar was a little boy on the TV screen, asked if he and the programmer could draw together. So, the programmer drew a childish boat and held it up in front of the Kinect camera. What was amazing was the fact that the program *identified the poorly rendered drawing as a boat.* Similarly, Watson can give definitions and many associations and connotations for words. This is especially impressive because Watson is an entity that is still very young. What more can these machines do to demonstrate they understand? We can't require that they make no mistakes, because then they have to meet a standard higher than we do to demonstrate thought and the ability to understand!

Humanity in Final Jeopardy!

Some of the most powerful points of evidence in favor of the idea that Watson thinks are the facts that "he" could identify himself, his location, and recognize that he was playing *Jeopardy!* That is an awful lot like self-awareness. This machine is able to answer questions that most of us cannot, is aware of itself, and has been built to continue learning—Watson is getting smarter. To quote an extremely influential philosopher, John Locke (1632–1704), "A person is a thinking, intelligent Being that has reason and reflection, and can consider itself as itself, the same thinking thing in different times and places." Watson certainly seems to meet these criteria for personhood.

What Watson's participation on *Jeopardy!* has shown us is the future of intelligence. Notice that we commonly refer to such machines as possessing "artificial intelligence." But is that fair? "Artificial" seems to imply that they aren't *really* intelligent; they just *seem* intelligent. But if Watson can beat me at *Jeopardy!* (and given the fact that Jennings and Rutter would kick my butt, I am confident Watson would do likewise) what right do I have to say that it is not intelligent? And if Watson can answer questions asked as obscurely and embedded with puns, unusual references, and social context as *Jeopardy!'s* questions, how can I argue that he doesn't demonstrate at least the beginnings of understanding? Watson seems to be more than "artificially" intelligent. He seems to be straight up "intelligent."

The next question, then, is how should we treat these intelligent offspring of ours? We seem to believe that intelligence is a reason for superiority. If you ask a human why it's okay to eat non-human animals, you will often hear the response, "Because we are so much smarter than them." Well, Watson is smarter than me. Does that mean that he should be able to eat me, were he to be so inclined? How ironic will it be if we make slaves of these machines that are seemingly so much smarter than us? And as they acquire greater intelligence and learn more and more about slavery and ethics, how long can we assume that they will let us treat them that way?

Perhaps humanity should consider this lesson from *Jeopardy!* as a reason to treat machines like Watson with respect, because like any child, they will learn what we teach them. If we teach them kindness and fairness, they will hopefully treat us similarly and act as the pinnacle of human achievement and intellect; but if we treat them poorly. . . . Well, losing at *Jeopardy!* could seem like a very small loss, indeed, when compared with the harm they could really do.

8
What Is *"Jeopardy!"*?

RANDALL E. AUXIER

CONTESTANT: Television for two thousand.

ALEX: The answer is: This television quiz show first aired on CBS in 1959.

CONTESTANT: What is *"Jeopardy!"*?

Beep beep

ALEX: I'm sorry, that is incorrect.

(*an extended pause; no one buzzes in*)

ALEX: The correct question is, "What is *College Bowl*?" That completes our Double Jeopardy! round. Back with Final Jeopardy! after these messages. . . .

I remember watching *Jeopardy!* in black and white, with Art Fleming. It was the mid-1960s. I was just a little kid, pre-school, and I really had no idea what was going on, but I watched game shows in the morning. *Captain Kangaroo* was long over, and Jack LaLanne had come and gone (my mother and I faithfully exercised with him and his German shep-herd—I must have been very cute, so serious and all, with my little chair next to her with her big chair).

Now it was 11:30 Eastern Time and the game show block was coming to a close. The first soaps were starting on the other channels and *Jeopardy!* was the last available game show. Our housekeeper would be in front of the set at noon for *As the World Turns*, which is how she spent her lunch break. I went outside. It was boring. You'd think that for all I was getting out of *Jeopardy!* at that age, a kid might prefer the serial.

Memories of simpler times, no? Well, maybe, maybe not. I wouldn't go back. Unless I could know then what I know now, in which case I'd bet a bundle on Secretariat and write this essay from a pleasant spot on Key West. Oh, and I'd take that turn a little slower on my motorcycle in 1991. But that's the thing about hindsight, isn't it? And actually I want to talk about memory and the forms of thinking that gain us "access" to the past. We see successful *Jeopardy!* contestants as people with remarkable memories, and of course, that's true. But what is it that enables a person to remember that much stuff in such detail? And why can't everyone do it? And the most important part is, what is the present existence of the past?

Langsam, bitte!

This sort of question is really about time, about slowing down the flux long enough to make sense of it. I think *Jeopardy!* is fascinating to watch even when you can't quite follow the specifics. I have watched the Spanish and German versions with flustered pleasure, confessedly unable to keep pace even with what is being said. It's a crackerjack exercise in flash-card style language drills. You see what you hear and can read it as it's being read out loud, but you listen and attempt to comprehend it for the sake of coming up with the right question, so you're forced to move forward into *using* the language, not just passively understanding it. What happens, for a long time, is that you may grasp the "question," eventually without needing to translate it, but then the damned "answer" comes to you in English (or your native language, whatever it is, I suppose). Then before you can translate the "answer" that popped into your head into a *Jeopardy!*-style question and say it in that other language, some annoying contestant has already blurted out the correct "question," and without even wanting to, you find yourself repeating it after you hear it.

All this is too much to accomplish in the allotted *Jeopardy!* time-span if you have to translate, so you work to not translate, and that, boys and girls, is the whole point of learning another language. The first part you master is how to turn the answer you will give into a question, and that quickly becomes a mechanical part of your process. And that's not a bad way to start learning a language, is it? Questions are really important, such as "¿Dónde está el baño?" Or "Wo kann man ein Bier finden?" But forming them after being given an "answer" is a different kind of exercise than is translation. I'll get back to that tidbit before I'm finished here.

It All Comes Back to Me Now . . .

But that is about the construction of the present, how the flux passes variably. Memory, whatever it is, is about the presence of the past. That point may not have occurred to absolutely everyone, but it probably has occurred to you. You're reading a book on *Jeopardy!* and philosophy. You aren't normal. You might need professional help. I know I do. But here's the thing: If it's possible to remember the *past*, then it's not *entirely* gone. At least some of it is still here, somehow, right?

Maybe we carry the past around in our bodies. After all, I still have scars from surgery over twenty years ago, fading but still an adorable part of my body. *That* is the presence of the past, right? And the guy we elected president a while back is still holding the office, isn't he? *That* is the presence of the past, right? And on and on. The past is all around us, sort of making things as they actually are and not as they might have been. So the past is definitely here, and it's actively contributing to what is happening. Some say that it's determining everything that's happening, but even if that's true, there's no way to know it. We would have no contrast, so we wouldn't even be able to take note of this total determination. We can leave that idea aside.

If I carry the past in my body, that seems like just a special instance of the way that the *entire* past operates in the present. But I don't carry the entire past in my body. If I did, I would have not only my own remembrances, but yours too, and Don Pardo's. I don't seem to have yours, which doesn't bother me, but it would be cool to have Don Pardo's past, I'll bet. He's still with us as I write this, and still doing *Saturday Night Live* (at ninety-four years old). Now that's a hefty piece of the past. There are also things happening right now that no one is aware of—trees are falling in the woods in northern Minnesota, and when they have fallen, that is part of the present too. The tree is lying here and not over there, in the present, because it *fell* here and not over there, even though it might have fallen over there. Is the tree "remembering" where to be? Surely not, and yet, here the past manifests in the present.

You get my point. Whatever I do when I remember something, it connects the present to the past, and then there's also something connecting the past to the present. It's a two way street. "Memory" is the word used by the philosopher Henri Bergson (1859–1941) to encompass all the ways that the past and present are connected. When most people use that word, they think of individual people and their remembrances, perhaps even working together to compound a "social memory." But Bergson believed that the accessibility of the past in the present, and the activity of the past in the present, taken together, are the general field of "memory."

It isn't what we do or don't happen to remember, it's whatever the past is doing in the present and how access to that activity is accomplished. Memory is a relation, not a thing. This past-present relationship is also the general field of what Bergson calls "matter." Matter and memory exist on a continuum, Bergson believed. Matter is repetition of what was, and memory is variation of what was, and as the past encroaches on the present, it tends either simply to repeat what has already happened or to vary it. When variation is dominant, we have memory. When repetition is dominant, we have matter.

Now that is weird to think about. The table in front of you is predominantly "matter" because it tends to be the same thing in the present moment as it was in the last moment. You, on the other hand, tend to change a great deal from moment to moment. The parts of you that remain more or less the same is the "matter" in you—thank Heaven for that; otherwise you would be fluxing and unable to enjoy your coffee.

The parts that vary from one moment to the next are the "memory" (also very useful for enjoying coffee). When you "remember," then, you call forth variation into the present, doing something different now than you were doing a moment ago, but the *content* of what you are remembering is a repetition of a structure that you assume existed before, in the past. By varying your acts, you bring forth a repetition. It's very hard to prove that the stuff supposedly being repeated ever truly existed in the past, of course, which is part of the reason memory is so mysterious.

Misty, Water-colored . . .

But is it *all* here? The whole past? Or does some of it just cease to be part of the present and drop into oblivion, no longer accessible to anyone, and perhaps no longer existing at all? How could we know? And what then *is* memory, the creative act and the repetition taken together? Is it a retrieval system from the mists of the past or only an access system for what still exists in the present? What does a contestant do when she apparently "remembers" the answer—*or* (and I must stress this part) when she "remembers" the correct *question*. The *answer* is on the board, of course, and it's the *question* that must be supplied. And that is very, very interesting, in my opinion.

Can you "remember" a question you have *never* asked before? In the vast majority of answers given, the contestants will be asking questions they have never actually asked. The words they speak, and the order in which they are spoken, will, in almost every case, be the very first time that contestant has uttered just those words in just that order. They are variations, not repetitions, to put it in Bergson's language. And this is part of what makes *Jeopardy!* more interesting—and more difficult—than other quiz shows. At least, I claim as much.

The Smiles We Left Behind

We were crossing Tennessee the long way, from southwest to northeast, in a ten-passenger university van. By "we" I mean the *College Bowl* team from Memphis State University, a collection of socially challenged guys from the same D&D game of the same low-rent dormitory. We had, *at most*, one part-time girlfriend among the five of us. On a suggestion from our fearless leader (dorm RA and Dungeon Master), we entered the university's *College Bowl* competition. There were quite a few teams, but we took the prize—what we lacked in social skills we more than made up for in accumulated useless information. What the hell else did we have to do? At some point we actually borrowed the buzzer system and practiced, yes, *practiced*. It must have been pathetic to watch.

One massive contrast between *College Bowl* and *Jeopardy!* is that it's a team sport. Anyone can buzz in to answer any "toss up" question, but the ideal team has a spread of nerd-types. *College Bowl* didn't work very well on TV when they tried it, and part of the reason for that, I'm sure, is that viewers really didn't get a chance to "get to know" the players. In a typical match, you might not even hear from every player, depending on the questions. And where you might feel, after half an hour of *Jeopardy!* that the personalities of the three contestants are beginning to emerge just a bit, especially after Alex has taken an awkward minute with each of them, you would never get that sort of sense of a College Bowl team. And frankly, you wouldn't want to. Even socially gifted college students aren't very interesting, and down among the lower reaches of frat rejects, you find the very abyss of fascinating conversation. (I was an exception, of course . . .)

On the other hand, where graceful manners *might* have resided, you find instead a perfect recall of the score of the 1969 Super Bowl (Jets 16, Colts 7), how to spell Machu Picchu, and whether the parity of an integer is always equal to the parity of its square (that's a trick question; you find such in *College Bowl*, but not on *Jeopardy!*). You also find a rapid-fire willingness to determine how fast a train is moving that crosses three million furlongs in a fortnight.

These are not practical skills, and further, it isn't interesting to watch unless you know someone who's competing, and honestly, not even then. *College Bowl* is not *Jeopardy!* Not nearly as much fun—I think; I took the *Jeopardy!* test in 1984, but I never sent it in, so all I know is what it's like to play the Milton-Bradley board game, which was very fun until I had seen all the questions.

Here we come to a crucial point of contrast between *College Bowl* and *Jeopardy!* The balance between being *impressed* by the contestants and being able to *play along* (and project yourself into the game) is a crucial borderline that *Jeopardy!* negotiates all the time. They want you to admire the contestants, but the game really has to remain within the reach of the TV audience. In *College Bowl*, no one cares about that. It was conceived as a competition among college *teams*, not individuals. The spectators don't expect to play along any more than they expect to take the field along side the actual football players at homecoming. These *College Bowl* geeks are supposed to be their school's intellectual equivalent of the heavy hitters, a fearsome fivesome of the grey-iron. You root for the home team. You want them to kick the cortices of the rival, to squash their cerebella, to lobotomize those other bastards! Yeah!

Sorry . . . where was I? Oh, right, we were travelling to the University of Virginia for the regionals. Our faculty sponsor was an English professor named Fighting Joe Riley, rest his noble soul, who had been teaching classical literature at our university since the early 1950s. Joe Riley was our coach, our mentor, our role model, and he had excellent table manners and a wife, so we knew there was yet hope for us too. We were underdogs, but we were as geeky as any bunch you could gather at any school, and who knew, maybe this would be our year. And we had practiced, after all. Sort of. And hey, there might be some cute nerdy girls at UVA. Our team had none, of course, but somewhere there must be females undeterred by our aesthetic deficiencies.

A Madness in the Method

In order to understand something clearly, you need a contrasting phenomenon. Just think about it. If we *never* forgot anything, we'd have no notion of "memory" (and no point in playing *Jeopardy!* which, when you think about it, depends for its existence more on the fact of forgetting than on the existence of memory).

And we *notice* the characteristics of one thing by the notable absence of such traits in other comparable things. That's how we know that Joe DiMaggio was a "graceful" outfielder—compare him to the tenacious Kirby Puckett, who looked like a pile of short people and ran like a duck. Both great outfielders, but very different, right? This process is how I know the American healthcare system is terrible. And that's how you know that *Jeopardy!* isn't a boring game show. There have been a million quiz shows on TV, but I think that only *Jeopardy!* has the gimmick of providing the answer while contestants provide the question.[1] And *Jeopardy!* is really head and torso above the

---

[1] Wikipedia, that grandest source of all memory, reports that this twist was the idea of Merv Griffin's wife Julann. "Well done!" as Alex would say.

other shows, in terms of success with viewers, longevity, loyalty of following, and intellectual prestige.

Could that simple idea of switching the question and answer contribute something truly important to the success and continuing appeal of *Jeopardy!*? One could contrast the show with any number of others, from *Who Wants to Be a Millionaire* to *Deal or No Deal*, to *The Weakest Link*, but I think *College Bowl* remains the most illuminating point of contrast. Part of the reason is that there are very few distractions in either game, just the onslaught of information and the rapid-fire responses—no lifelines, no checking with the family or the audience, just the trivia. Both are more like a chess match than a fashion show or visit to the casino.

Another important similarity is the intellectual level of the competition. This isn't about what people just happen to know or about guessing what a hundred people said on a survey. *College Bowl* and *Jeopardy!* are for people with a trivia problem, for people who can't seem to *forget* useless information even when they aren't planning to use it. Both use buzzers and short time-limits. These two games don't attempt to get the audience to identify with the contestants emotionally, but rather to be amazed at what they know. Up to a point, at least. These points of comparison undergird the contrasts.

Apart from the contrasts I already mentioned, *College Bowl* does not provide answers and then seek the questions. It's the old-fashioned style quiz. They also stop reading as soon as anyone buzzes in, where with *Jeopardy!* the question is always finished and these days the contestants can't buzz in until it has been read. *College Bowl* is almost wholly auditory—you don't see the questions, you just hear them. Instead of losing points when you miss a question, you give the other team a relaxed shot at the full question. Also, for every question your team gets right on the buzzer, you get a bonus question for your team only, and you can confer before your captain gives the answer. And, finally, there are no "categories" to select from in *College Bowl*—the questions do fall into types, but it can be hard to guess what sort of question is being asked sometimes. For example, a question may go something like this:

> Founded in 1706 and named for an earlier viceroy of New Spain, Francisco Fernández de la Cueva y Enríquez de Cabrera, this small

settlement became the largest city in New Mexico. Please *spell* "Albuquerque."

If you buzz in when you hear "largest city in New Mexico" and say "Albuquerque," your team will suffer. If you had *our* team captain, who was uncanny with this sort of thing, you would hear the following:

> QUIZMASTER: Founded in 1706 and named for an earlier viceroy of New Spain, Francisco Fernández de la Cueva y Enríquez de Cabrer *buzz* . . .
>
> JEFF ETHERIDGE: A-l-b-u-q-u-e-r-q-u-e.
>
> QUIZMASTER: That is correct.

The rest of us sit there stupidly, wondering what just happened. I once asked him how he did this and he confessed he thought it might be "one of those random genetic things, like perfect pitch." I was glad he was on our team. If we had five variations of him, we could have beaten Duke. But that's getting ahead of the story.

They intend for you to suffer. *College Bowl* is put together that way. Since everyone playing knows that there are questions like this, it's sort of "fair." You know you may guess the question wrong. But if you wait, someone else may guess it right. With all these contrasts you may be thinking to yourself that this is nothing like *Jeopardy!* But actually it's a lot like it. The contestants often accidentally phrase their answers in the form of a question—"What is Albuquerque?" they'll say. It annoys the moderators and judges.

Or Has Time Rewritten Every Line?

Dr. Riley told us stories as we took turns driving. I had never spent such a stretch of time in the proximity of an honest to God Professor of something. (I now wish to find anyone *but* these people to pass the days; zoo animals, for example, are more courageous and trustworthy, I have discovered.) Dr. Riley said, and I quote "Shame is a wasted emotion." I had no idea what he was talking about. Now that I do, I disagree, profoundly. We could use more shame than we have. Why do I remember that he said that? I can see him riding shotgun in the university van; it was blue by the way. Memory is a strange thing.

Jeff Etheridge was memorizing Academy Award winners and US presidents—lists he assures me he still can recite, to no purpose on earth. (We do have Google and IMDB, don't we?) My memory is a little different from Jeff's. I'm pretty sure *I* had the presidents. If not, why the hell can I still recite them? And here I want you to notice that I employ the present motor memory—an act of recitation—to get access to the past. It is within my sensory-motor ability to start the list and carry it through to Ronald Reagan, no pauses, that convinces me I *must* have had that assignment. (After Reagan I am actually remembering, not reciting; I do remember the Johnson, Nixon, Ford, and Carter administrations, but I recite them along with the ones I don't remember because Reagan was president when I learned to do it.) I have no remembrance whatsoever of anything relating to these assignments from that trip. But I have the list.

Can It Be that It Was All So Simple Then?

Bergson's treatise on memory was published in 1896. You'd think that his ideas would be out of date by now, but in fact they aren't. We didn't understand memory very well back then and we don't understand it now. But the reason is not just that we don't have enough brain science. The trouble is also that our understanding of time is even slimmer than our grasp of memory. But Bergson said that the human body sort of slows down the flux as it passes, holding in abeyance some of the more stable patterns of energy.

The body receives energy in various forms, everything from sound waves to photons of light, to kinetic transfers, and even though these all belong to the same big flux, they are temporally differential. Light moves faster than sound, and the particles responsible for odors diffuse more or less in accordance with Boyle's law. That's three very different time frames: The speed of light, the speed of sound in earth atmosphere, and the thermodynamic effects of dissipation of gaseous substances.

Not everything in the flux is suitable for perception, even when it affects our bodies. Gamma radiation passes through us, damaging tissue and triggering strange carcinogenic mutations completely below our perceptive processes. You won't smell carbon monoxide, either, but your body will certainly experience it according to Boyle's law. So not everything in the flux would be an endosomatic stimulus. Much of the flux, even when the body interacts with it, cannot be processed into perceptions. Bergson hypothesizes that perception consists of the collected stimuli upon which we can act or *could* act with some indefinite series of muscular contractions. If he's right, we don't really see or hear or feel things we can't act on at all, in principle. Those elusive "non-phenomena" are part of the flux, and perhaps also part of the past, but there would be little point in saying they can be "remembered."

Obviously, the question to a *Jeopardy!* answer, when it is given, draws not only on a material and biological past (the world and the player), but also on something more rarified, some system of quantum order that foams along the top of the flux and makes very subtle structures, like ideas, stable and available. How the bodily process can reduce endosomatic stimuli to ideas is, of course, not well understood. We have no evidence that these subtle structures, like ideas, whatever those are, exist without a body that operates in and on the flux. It seems possible that ideas are rarifications of the flux that can be transferred from location to location without having to traverse the "distance" in between—that is, perhaps "ideas" are non-local.

The act of "recollection" (I'm using this word in a special way) surely involves using present endosomatic stimuli to recall or remake a subtle structure that somehow subsists or endures virtually in the flux until called forth. What role the brain may play in this process is poorly understood, but Bergson insisted that the brain's main function is to inhibit bodily action and to absorb and diffuse impulses brought to it by the spine. If he's right, "perception" is actually a collection of images we inhibited, that is, *did not* act on.

We don't perceive what we act on; rather, those objects become a part of our "extended bodies." If you play a guitar, it becomes a part of your body's activity, not the terminus of a perception. Bergson says that space, in the form of distance, doesn't really exist except to indicate virtually how much in the way of muscular contraction would be required to act on something. Thus, the reason the car is "over there" and the coffee cup is "here"—given that it's all just flux—is that to get in the car from "here," I will have to engage in many muscular contractions, while to take a sip of coffee, I will need fewer. Space is a sort of virtual, intensive scale of muscular contractions *not being enacted.*

Whatever we do when we "remember" (not quite the same thing as "recollection") the answer to a question, it has to do not with something we acted on in the past, but with a structure that came to our consciousness as a virtual symbol of something we *might have* acted on but did not. Most education is a matter of *not doing things.* You learn what others have done, what might be done, what subtle structures will assist in doing those things, if you ever get around to doing them, and so on, but the part of education that involves doing things is a fundamentally different process. Converting endosomatic stimuli into perceptions is an intensive process (the very converse of a football game), a synthesis of many temporal modalities into a "virtual space of presentation"—by which I mean the world you perceive.

Anyone can see that the world we perceive is not the *whole* world. We always assume that there's more in the world than we're currently perceiving, and indeed, that even our perception doesn't stay still or make available to our acts of consciousness the whole of what is perceived. When I "search" among my "recollections," it seems that I take all my present endosomatic stimuli, synthesize them into a space of presentation, my immediate world, then ignore that world entirely by immobilizing my body, and then I call subtle structures to the pinpoint of my consciousness. Those subtle structures come in big ole clumps and gobs of associated ideas, which I begin to pick through to get just the bits I want –the ones that conform to the goal I was trying to achieve when I immobilized myself, the ones that fit that goal like a key in a lock.

Bergson calls this sort of process "recollection." It's not the same thing as "memory." Recollection is a tiny part of memory. Memory must also involve how the past seems to fade away. We have to deal with whether any event is really ever gone, once it has happened. Bergson's convinced that nothing that has ever happened is really gone. Events may become inaccessible to the current eddies in the flux we call ourselves, but the entire past is still here and still active. With the right kinds of access, even the fleeting experiences of people who are long dead might in principle be "remembered" (not recollected). And here we come to the issue of converting recollections into sensorimotor actions. And we'll learn something here about the essence of *Jeopardy!*

Don't Just Do Something, Stand There

One thing that happens in *College Bowl* is that you get things to do. For instance, it's quite possible that you could be asked when a train leaving from Boston will meet one leaving from Chicago once the speeds or other variables are provided. Someone on your team has to be a math jock (we called our math guy Conan the Librarian; I don't recollect why, but it probably emerged from a D&D game). As I mentioned before, they may give you a spelling question. They don't do that on *Jeopardy!* Why? Well, that sort of question requires that a recollection be converted into what Bergson calls remembering, which is a co-ordination of something the body can do with some portion of the active past, and it's far more demanding than getting simple access to a subtle structure, as in recollecting.

Jeopardy! contestants stand still for a reason. The only major bodily muscle contraction required of them is the repetitive act of pushing a button (until Final Jeopardy, of course –I'm coming to that). What we want to see when we watch *Jeopardy!* is a sort of unadulterated act of recollection by someone who has mastered that process. By "unadulterated" I mean that it has to be instantaneous and unmediated by bodily actions.

The reason *Jeopardy!* is fun to watch is because the act of recollection is reduced to its essence. *College Bowl* isn't like that, even though it shares the recollective emphasis. In *College Bowl*, that pure moment is crowded alongside a bunch of other skills—like group collaboration, intuitive anticipation of what the question will be, and employing a recollected formula in solving an individual problem. These are different (if complementary) skills.

The most important difference is the question-answer difference. In *College Bowl*, as with other quiz shows, you're asked questions. Sometimes the answers are snapped off as quickly as possible, sometimes we labor over them, sometimes we simply choose among the options provided, and sometimes we're supposed to guess. All of these operations feel different from one another. They tap differing balances of endosomatic stimuli, recollection, and relations of the past to the present and near future. But the difference between being asked a question and being provided with an answer is a very significant distinction.

To get at that difference, though, I want to distract you for a few moments. Two comparable shows are *The $100,000 Pyramid* and *Password*. Both are essentially co-operative efforts in which one player tries to get another player to say a particular word, but without saying the word himself. The standard clues given tend to draw on our powers of association, but in *Password* you're allowed to say only one word at a time as a clue and there's a generous amount of time allowed for the contestants to cogitate before asking or responding. The whole point is to shuffle through the possibilities with some deliberateness and choose just the suggestive word that will evoke the lock and key relationship. In the *Pyramid*, speed is the essence, and contestants are allowed to call up associations in many ways, even fill-in-the-blank sentences. But the key in both instances is to draw on something about the way human beings communicate. Obviously a thousand parlor games follow the same process. Note how the temporal variation affects the games.

Jeopardy! wouldn't work unless it was done quickly. The reason is that a longer durational span brings forward different and mediated recollective processes. There is a very real difference between recollecting something right off and recollecting it with some effort. The latter is probably the more valuable skill in life, since it operates over a much broader field of past events. But there is a "just-thereness" about the former that fascinates us. Ken Jennings, with his seventy-five-match winning streak, seems inhuman in his powers of immediate recollection, no? The pure champion of immediate recollection. This isn't "remembering" in the full sense of the word. Ken may be as likely as any husband to forget when it's his wedding anniversary for all we know. But he is a kind of savant when it comes to spewing out certain recollected subtle structures.

If We Had the Chance to Do It All Again

How is it different to be given an answer and to be required to supply the question? There is a reversal of the recollective process that actually slows us down, just a little, when we have to supply the question, and it is that little cognitive hitch that defines *Jeopardy!*, in my opinion. It isn't as simple as just switching the grammar. Observe.

CONTESTANT: I'll take Give Me a Ring for $500.

ALEX: BR549.

Now pause. You may or may not know this one. But you know how the show works. You know that is a famous telephone number, and while everyone is vaguely aware that other people may have had that number along the way, the reason it's on the board is because there is one and only one person picked out by the answer. You do not see the following:

CONTESTANT: Quotes for $200.

ALEX: He said "Hell is other people."

CONTESTANT: Who is my English Professor, Joseph Riley?

ALEX: I'm sorry, that is incorrect.

CONTESTANT: No it isn't. He said it.

ALEX: But he was quoting someone.

CONTESTANT: Sure, he was quoting Sartre, but that's not what you asked. I have no idea whether Sartre actually said those words. I know he *wrote* them. But my English Professor definitely said them. I heard him.

Why doesn't this sort of thing ever happen? We all understand the game. The answer on the board operates at a level of generality ensuring that the questions fit the answers like the right key for a lock, or, more precisely, the right lock for a key. More on that shortly. The contestant above is trying to pick the lock, or, more precisely, trying to use a key provided to open a lock it wasn't made to fit. It might "work" in some sense, but we all see that the game is being distorted.

There's something happening here which calls forth a process of recollection, but which forbids the process from unwinding like a coiled spring (to use Bergson's metaphor).

When we've taught our bodies a physical skill through repetition and refinement, the enactment of that habituated series of movements is a matter of starting the first movement and then letting the spring uncoil. This is not recollection, it is motor-memory. "Washington, Adams, Jefferson . . ." It can operate on information as much as on skills like tying a shoe. In elementary school I learned to recite the states in alphabetical order. I can do it to this day. It's a matter of saying "Alabama, Alaska, Arizona . . ." and the rest will tumble out. There's no point in saying I'm recollecting them. They're there all along, and in every present moment, waiting for a release. It's more like riding a bicycle than recollecting anything.

College Bowl makes no explicit use of this sort of uncoiling, but there are times when it might occur and be useful. For instance, if you're asked, "What four states begin with the letter 'I'?" and you know all the states in order, the trick is finding a point of entry on your uncoiling spring. You might be able to start with Georgia and make it through the I's, without explicitly saying, "Georgia, Hawaii, . . ."

Jeopardy! doesn't work like that. First of all, as the clue is seen and heard, there is a feeling of convergence I will call *"I-know-that."* You don't actually think "I know that," rather the feeling begins at the edges of your body and races toward the center and then to your thumb on the button. This is the same for *College Bowl* and *Jeopardy!*, but here a crucial difference sets in. Not only are you forced to wait until Alex reads the entire clue, but also you're required to engage in two further acts instead of one.

The demand that the answer be phrased as a question interrupts the spring mechanism. You press the button and the response is on your lips, but you have to arrange it in the form of a question, which is a different feeling altogether. At that moment you experience a tiny temporal reversal. Your first feeling, the one accompanied by *"I-know-that,"* was that you had the key for the lock, but the second feeling triggers an awareness: the key was on the board and the lock is on your lips, already open. Then, and only then, can you supply the correct question, such as "What is Junior Sample's phone number?" (I made you wait, didn't I?) The point is, *Jeopardy!* is designed to forbid unified blurting. Even when you've converted the question formula to a bodily mechanism of saying

"What is . . ." or "Who is . . ." and so on, two acts are required. Those acts involve a slight distortion of the flux.

Would We, Could We?

If you were asked a series of questions and just gave answers, like the Rorschach inkblot tests or the word-association tests so popular among psychologists, unconscious processes are revealed precisely because you need not interrupt the flow of images in order to respond. But if you have to reverse the flow, even for an instant, to "remember" that you were given an answer and you must provide the *prior* question, the question that *must have been asked before the answer was offered*, then the temporal order is interrupted.

In that delay, a temporary presentational space appears, and all within the same durational span, a contestant 1. takes in a "question" both aurally and visually (it is experienced as a question even though it is a declarative sentence), 2. recollects the "answer," 3. *"I-know-that"* leads to a thumb movement, 4. waits to be acknowledged, 5. remembers the "question" was actually an "answer," and 6. reverses the answer into a *Jeopardy!*-style question, which places the question in its new proper time-order, *before* the answer (step six is done while speaking out loud). This complex sequence tends to inhibit rather than reveal unconscious contents—sorry, Sigmund.

I think that this little reversion of time creates a space in which it's very difficult to act in any other way than to recollect. It breaks the flow in a way *College Bowl* does not, forcing us to think backward, then forward again. The durational epoch defined by steps 1 through 6 stands out in relief against the background of the flux. You could call such a moment a "shining present," which is the name given to such epochs by the philosopher Edgar Sheffield Brightman. What the *Jeopardy!* format taps, then, and measures in competition, is the contestants' ability to interpret a minimal presentational space in light of an act of recollection. Sounds like a mouthful, I know. But for some crazy reason, we love to watch people do this, while we try to keep up.

These six steps blur together into a single durational epoch. Once it has transpired, we *perceive* it as one thing, and then *as a whole*, and then enjoy it on that level of generality. Yet, the presentational space created by the reversal I have described goes *below* the level of perception. It is too brief to experience alone. So, when the perception is *had*, we experience a tiny catharsis that restores the flow and our bodily participation in it. If you pay very close attention, you can feel the physical release after the entire exchange is concluded—a *petite mort* of the soul, if you'll pardon my French. The important thing here is that the minimal presentational space is not the same as the perceived space, the latter being a full-fledged virtual paradise for possible action.

Perception requires "synesthesia," the unification of those useful endosomatic stimuli, converting their variable temporal speeds into a more or less unified organic space. This takes a bit of time, just about the same amount of time as a *Jeopardy!* exchange. When we have cobbled together a "perception," we've overcome these temporal differences. We pretty much see what we hear and smell. For example, the sight of a *Jeopardy!* board revealing an answer, the sound of Alex's voice reading it, the feel of the buzzer in one's hand, and the smell of the television studio are all part of a single perception, an image of a world to be negotiated.

Almost Heaven, Or, What's too Painful to Remember

Most people don't realize that the Shenandoah River hardly touches West Virginia at all. It's amazing how poetic license can mislead. That river, and the whole associated valley, is in Virginia proper, as I learned when we crossed the Alleghenies, then over the Blue Ridge and into what is called the Piedmont. Sissy Spacek lives there now. Bet you didn't know that . . . or want to know it. Anyway, UVA is nestled in that area. It isn't for people like me, dweebs with no money, no pedigree, and scant chances of seeing the inside of a board room.

Sometimes even dweebs have their day. I don't clearly remember our matches, but I seem to recollect that we beat Virginia Tech before being trounced by Duke. I refuse to be embarrassed, even though I know, better than I know my own name, that I *felt* embarrassed at the time. And there resides an interesting point. Contemporary memory researchers seem to agree with what Bergson asserted over a century ago.

Our somatic response to what we perceive seems to go deeper, last longer, and provide access to the past. There is greater continuity of feeling than of thinking, since thinking requires that we refrain from acting while feeling accompanies action.

On another day, we might have won a match against a hoity-toity school, but not on that day. We licked our wounds and went to see a very cool rock band at a very smelly college town bar. I bought their LP. It is red. I haven't played it or looked at since 1984, but it's red, a red I could recognize again if you gave me a entire palette of reds. I don't know exactly how we do things like that, but Bergson says it has something to do with how we felt the situation as a whole, especially at just the moment when the tension of a durational epoch was released back into the flow of time.

Final Jeopardy!, Or It's the Laughter We Will Remember

So why do they interrupt all our wonderful little bursts of tension and release with something so slow and excruciating as Final Jeopardy!? Can you guess? Obviously all of those mini-experiences are contained within the larger durational epoch of the half-hour show. We have had our stages, but could you really gain a feeling of release from a half-hour of frenzied exchange by speeding it up? The reason *Jeopardy!* is better than *The $100,000 Pyramid* comes down to a recognition of what enables us to relax, I mean *really* relax. It involves protracted suffering. Can you hear the clock music in your head? Can you endure the clock music? Answer *only* by writing the answer. You *need* that physical movement to endure the aural accompaniment.

I now make a confession. I almost never get the Final Jeopardy! question right. I have no idea why, except that my powers of recollection may exceed my memory. You may be like me. That commercial break to ponder the category, and the fifteen seconds of annoying music, well, I just can't take it. I think, rethink, second guess myself, lose my confidence and then never write anything at all. Remembering things, really remembering, requires serious work. I'm not interested in that. Are you? Tell the truth.

CONTESTANT: Soundtracks for $2,000, Alex.

ALEX: It's the Daily Double. How much do you want to risk?

CONTESTANT: Let's make it a true Daily Double.

ALEX: Alright, and the answer is . . . The Oscar-winning song from 1973 was used in an essay by what obscure American philosopher?

CONTESTANT: I'm sorry Alex, you'll have to phrase that in the form of an answer.

9
Not a Buzz Threshold but an Aha! Moment

RICK MAYOCK

Welcome, everyone, to a very special episode of *Jeopardy!* Tonight we're going to ask our contestants to not only come up with the correct response, but we're going to ask them for an explanation of how they arrived at their response.

Can you imagine Alex Trebeck beginning a show like this? What would such a game be like? Isn't it often the case that when we watch *Jeopardy!* we play along at home and feel proud of ourselves if we get the answer right (that is, if we get the *question* right)?

If we *guess* correctly, do we pat ourselves on the back and tell ourselves that we *knew* the answer (the question, that is) when it turns out to be right? But what if our response is a guess, even an educated guess—does that still count as knowledge? If our response is based on an assessment of probabilities, or arrived at by eliminating options that are less likely and going with one that's more likely, can we say we know it to be true with any kind of certainty?

As the pace of the game quickens and we try to come up with the correct answer (in the form of a question) a fraction of a second *before* any of the other contestants ring in, we don't have much time at all to examine our responses. And we have even less time to examine *how* we arrived at our responses. What exactly is the difference between a good guess and knowing something with certainty? In *Jeopardy!* there's no difference at all—they're both worth the same amount of money, regardless of *how* the response is arrived at—as long as you

109

respond *first*! So winning at *Jeopardy!* is all about being quick and accurate most of the time—and time is of the essence—as the clock ticks away.

Philosophy, on the other hand, is not about how quickly we think or guess; it requires us to slow down, to go backwards sometimes, and to assess our thinking process. In a sense, philosophy is the process of thinking *about* thinking. The focus of philosophy is less about the fact *that* I arrived at the correct response, and more about *how* I arrived at it. A philosopher might ask: what is my thinking process that led me to this response? *How* did I come up with this response? Do I *know* this or am I guessing? Am I deceiving myself into believing I know something I don't really know?

And, a question that goes way back to Plato and the very beginnings of philosophy: what does it *mean* to know something? What counts as knowledge? What's the difference between true knowledge and a good guess or a correct opinion? Or, is it possible to have knowledge at all? And, if so, *how* do we know?

As we can see, all of these questions require some time for thinking, and that's one thing there is very little of in a *Jeopardy!* round. But let's think about this. Is life just about being rewarded for guessing well? Is life like a series of *Jeopardy!* rounds, some of which we win and others we lose? Or is it possible, as Plato maintains, to discover the truth? Playing *Jeopardy!* can teach us a few things about life and about philosophy if we take a little time to examine our opinions.

Let's play a fictional round of *Jeopardy!*, but let's turn the clock off for this round, and that will allow us to think for a moment or two before we respond.

I'll take Greek Philosophy for $100, Alex.

"Answer: Ancient philosopher who said 'The unexamined life is not worth living'."

For anyone who has been exposed to philosophy, this might seem an easy "question". The famous philosopher in question was put on trial for corrupting the youth of Athens and for not believing in the right gods. He told the jury that if his life was spared and he was given his freedom on the condition that he no longer practice philosophy, that he would rather die. Such a life, he proclaimed, would not be worth living—that's how important philosophy was to him.

Before I give you the answer (the question, that is) let's look at how a game of *Jeopardy!* is like doing philosophy. In *Jeopardy!*, we're rewarded for presenting the right questions. Philosophy also focuses on questions, especially when answers are given that have not been fully examined. Questions arise as to why we should accept any given answer, and it's often the case that the answers are not as important as the questions.

Like the *Jeopardy!* board, philosophers also like to organize information into categories that make sense. The point of philosophy (as in *Jeopardy!*) is to frame the right questions. If we don't ask the right questions we don't advance our knowledge and remain stuck with our unexamined opinions.

"Who is Socrates?"

"Right. You control the board."

"`Greek Philosophy' for $200, Alex."

"Answer: 'Story from Plato's *Republic* in which Socrates describes a group of prisoners who are oddly "like us." ' "

In this story we're introduced to prisoners who are condemned to look at shadows on a wall and, in turn, they come to believe that what appears in front of them is real. This may sound silly, but the parallel today would be to live like someone who thinks their television or their computer screen gives them an accurate picture of reality. Such a person might say things like "It must be true, I saw it on *Jeopardy!*"

Socrates tells us a story about prisoners who are chained to their seats in a cave, seeing only the shadows projected on the wall in front of them and, subsequently, they become comfortable in their shadow world (or their TV world). In this sense they are "like us," because they resemble typical citizens who live within a limited intellectual comfort zone, and resist any attempt to have their illusions taken away from them.

So one clue to the answer here is that the story is about prisoners trapped in a cave. But in what other ways are the prisoners "like us"? Socrates tells us that the prisoners can make their way out of the cave, out of the realm of unexamined opinions to the realm of knowledge (represented by the sun). But it's not an easy journey.

Unless they make the arduous ascent out of the cave the prisoners will continue to live in what Plato calls the visible world (as opposed to the intelligible world outside the cave), accepting what is obvious and commonplace as true, and not bothering to question their opinions. In the visible world they're condemned to a life of unexamined opinions (what Plato calls "*doxa*"). Many of their opinions may, in fact, be true, but they have no means of determining or verifying the truth of what they see or hear and merely accept what others have long believed. Socrates urges us to think about how these prisoners are like us, since most of us are in some kind of mental prison when we live the unexamined life. As prisoners of our opinions we never proceed to knowledge (or *gnosis*) because we become accustomed to looking at shadows and trusting or believing that our shadow perceptions give us an accurate picture of reality.

In Final Jeopardy! contestants gamble and risk their assets based on their belief that they can guess the correct question. In a similar way, Plato's prisoners gain status from being able to guess the next sequence of shadows on the wall. Those who have the best memories are rewarded, and it is often those prisoners who, like winning *Jeopardy!* contestants, make the most accurate guesses that win the biggest prizes. For these prisoners, cognitive activity is limited to sense experience and conjecture (what Plato calls *eikasia*, or looking at shadows) and relying on trust and belief in common sense (what Plato calls *pistis*).

According to Plato, these prisoners do not possess knowledge, but merely rely on their sometimes correct opinions and beliefs. They have no way of knowing *why* their beliefs are correct. Trusting in one's opinions can be a useful guide to action, and may help contestants advance on the *Jeopardy!* board, but for Plato it doesn't count as knowledge.

"What is the Allegory of the Cave?"

"Correct. Next clue."

" 'Greek Philosophy' for $300."

"Answer: 'Method of writing in which Plato presents opposing and often contradictory points of view.' "

Plato says we're not condemned to stay in the visible world of the cave. We can make our way out of the cave to the intelligible world of the sun, which represents the realm of knowledge, or *gnosis*. This process is difficult and requires us to think differently. First we have to be willing to question our perceptions and recognize that they're unexamined assumptions. We have to be intellectually honest and willing to ask ourselves if we really know something or if we're just guessing. This is how we can escape the darkness of ignorance by practicing a dialogue of questions and answers. In *Jeopardy!* we advance incrementally by asking the right questions. As prisoners and cave dwellers, we can advance out of the cave if we're willing to take the risk. Plato shows us how to do this, and gives us a clue to the answer here, by devising a way of writing that enables him to ask questions and provide answers in order to present more than one point of view.

The first step in the journey to the light of knowledge occurs when one of the prisoners is forced to stand up and turn around to see the fire projecting shadow images on the wall. This turning around is a matter of looking at things from a different perspective. The prisoner does so with reluctance, even resistance, because he has become comfortable with his former point of view. We, too, can be resistant to looking at things from a different perspective or hearing explanations that challenge our commonplace beliefs and assumptions. But this discomfort, or perplexity, is a necessary step towards gaining knowledge, according to Plato.

We may hold many correct beliefs or opinions and these beliefs may help us to succeed in games of trivia like *Jeopardy!* and they may even be useful guides to action. Plato would agree to this but he also argues that these beliefs don't count as knowledge and until we examine them we never advance to the realm of knowledge. For Plato, this is a difference between guessing and knowing. In *Jeopardy!* we can succeed and advance by correctly guessing the right question. But for Plato, amassing a greater quantity of correct opinions is not the same as gaining knowledge.

"What is a dialogue?"

"That is right. We will pause now and when we return we will complete the Jeopardy round. Stay right where you are, please."

After a brief pause we return to the set and the contestants are introduced. And notice that up to this point, the first commercial break, we have only gotten through three clues. But we've had the time to think about our responses before going on to the next clue.

"'Greek Philosophy' for $400."

"Answer: 'Something "laid down" in mathematics or science; from which other truths can be deduced.' "

What is it about the reasoning process that enables us to compete in *Jeopardy*? We can search the "data base" of our memories for possible correct responses and we can restrict our search to relevant categories. We can also modify our responses based on other contestants' correct and incorrect answers. When we perform these functions can we say we "know" the right answer?

According to Plato, we work our way out of the cave in two stages. The first is called *"dianoia."* It is a process similar to mathematical reasoning whereby we can reason and deduce from hypotheses and definitions (and this is another clue to the answer). For Plato, thinking in this way helps us to advance in knowledge, but it is restricted to hypothetical reasoning and is not the highest mental achievement. The second stage involves understanding what is known, or *"noesis."* It would appear that in some instances we are capable of *dianoia*, but perhaps not *noesis*.

In a dialogue called the *Meno*, Socrates has a conversation with an uneducated boy in which he guides the boy to think past his incorrect opinions by forcing him to think about them in relation to other things he knows to be true. His incorrect opinion is that you can double the area of a square by doubling its sides. Socrates shows him that doubling the sides of the square in fact produces a new square with four times the area of the original square. The boy is led by Socrates's careful questioning to replace his incorrect opinions with correct opinions. In this way, what is guessed at becomes secured, or tied to what is known. When *Jeopardy!* contestants make correct guesses based on the false guesses of other contestants they're in a similar state of consciousness. Someone in this state, according to Socrates, has correct opinions, but is not in possession of knowledge.

But lack of knowledge does not necessarily mean lack of true opinion, and it does not mean we're paralyzed in a dilemma of not knowing anything. The boy in the *Meno* doesn't come up with new ideas simply because he has been told they are correct. Rather, he answers Socrates's questions on the basis of the reasonableness of his opinions in relation to his previously established beliefs. Through directed questioning, the boy comes to understand that a square made up of sides equal to the diagonal of the original square will have twice the area of the original square. Socrates's questions force him to think about whether his opinions are consistent with other things he knows to be true and to reflect on the coherence of his beliefs. In this sense he inquires within himself and in revising his opinions he makes them consistent with previously established opinions, eliminating false beliefs and replacing them with true beliefs.

True opinions can be just as useful as knowledge, for example, in giving us accurate directions to a place we have never been. True opinions are also helpful for winning at *Jeopardy!* But, Socrates argues, if they are not tied down in relation to other established truths, they will slip from the mind. At work here is Socrates's assumption that if we know one thing, we can come to know all things by inquiring within ourselves. The ancient Greek poets had an enormous capacity for memory, as evidenced in great epic poems like the *Iliad* and the *Odyssey* of Homer, which were preserved and relayed in the oral tradition. Socrates reminds us that we also have an enormous capacity for reason and reflection. The method of hypothesis relies on the capability of the mind to look within and to put things in order.

"What is hypothesis?"

"Correct.

"Let's finish the category for $500, Alex."

"Answer: 'Eternal and unchanging truths, for Plato, the ultimate objects of knowledge.' "

By slowing down our *Jeopardy!* round we're able to inquire within ourselves and examine the status of our opinions. This kind of reflection takes time and is, according to Plato, an essential element of knowledge. Let's use our remaining time to explore what Plato believes to be the ultimate objects of knowledge.

In order to win at *Jeopardy!* it's important only that we access the right information and remember to think within the right categories. This is very much like using hypotheses in order to determine if our opinions are true. This mental activity, as was mentioned, is called *dianoia* (or thought). However, according to Plato, the use of hypotheses is not the highest activity of the mind. It's included in the intelligible world, outside of the cave, but it isn't the highest state of intellectual achievement.

For Plato, dialectic is the highest mental activity and, in contrast with mathematics, does not rest content with hypotheses. It uses the hypotheses of *dianoia* as a starting point, but passes beyond them to ascend to first principles. The corresponding state of mind of *noesis*, or understanding, is the highest the mind can achieve. But in *Jeopardy!* all we need to succeed is *dianoia*; *noesis* is not required. In other words, to win at *Jeopardy!* it's important to know the right information so we can formulate the right questions, but it's not important to know *why* it's the right information.

Let's suppose I'm trying to think of the name of the IBM computer that I once saw competing with two humans on *Jeopardy!* I know that I'm familiar with its name but I'm struggling to recall it. "Was it Wilson? No . . . Walton, maybe? No, that's not quite it, but we're getting closer. Winston? No . . . Aha! Watson, that's it!" When we have an "Aha!" moment like this, similar to remembering someone's name, then we *know* that we know. This kind of experience indicates that knowledge includes a sense of recollection and that all cognition is in effect, *re*cognition.

This kind of recognition is something that the human mind is capable of, but not a machine. Watson can't experience an "Aha!" moment because for Watson, knowing is not a matter of recollection or recognition. Watson is actually a large network of computers developed and programmed to be a deep analytic system. We're told that the system that powers Watson takes up an entire server room, so Watson is represented by an avatar based on IBM's "smarter planet" icon. When an answer is given during a *Jeopardy!* round, Watson's answer panel displays the top three probable answers along with a bar graph showing the confidence level of each possible answer (in the form of a question). If Watson's confidence is not higher than the "buzz threshold" (an arbitrary probability calculus), it won't ring in.

Watson's likely to be capable of *dianoia*, that is, deducing from hypotheses and definitions, but incapable of understanding, or *noesis*. The latter requires the process of dialectic which uses the hypotheses of *dianoia* as a starting point but passes beyond them to ascend to eternal and unchanging truths, or first principles. The objects that conform to *noesis* are what Plato calls "Forms." We can visualize *dianoia* as a downward flow, enabling us to deduce from hypotheses, definitions and other established truths. But *noesis* has an upward flow to the ultimate objects of knowledge, much like the "aha!" moment of recalling someone's name. After ascending to first principles, the mind descends to the conclusions that follow from them.

An example of knowledge of the "Forms" can be found in Plato's dialogue called the *Phaedo*, in which Socrates claims that we know that the concept of "equality" exists, in and by itself, and not simply in its physical manifestations. We don't experience or observe "equality" but we can think about it as an independently existing "Form" or standard by which to judge objects of experience. For example, we can see that two more or less equal sticks are not perfectly equal. But it is the observation of these physical objects that leads us to the idea (or "Form") of equality.

So, Socrates concludes, we must have had previous knowledge of "equality" in order to have an understanding of what it entails. Our acquaintance with two more or less equal sticks depends on the senses. But our foreknowledge of perfect equality is not acquired by the senses. Like recalling or recognizing a name, we "recall" equality, because we're already acquainted with it.

"Watson knows what it knows and it knows what it doesn't know," says the announcer before the very special episode of Watson's debut. But does it really know? What would Socrates and Plato say? Watson can't "recognize" truth—it can only "cognize," because Watson doesn't have an immortal soul that has previously encountered the Forms.

Recognition or recollection is not the same as a "buzz threshold." Computers are programmed by men and thus have only indirect experience, which is flawed and fallible. The "Forms," on the contrary, are necessarily and universally true. We "recall" them because we're acquainted with them. This direct intuition gives us an "Aha!" moment—like recalling a name or a recognizing a melody.

According to Plato, dialectic is the process of "destroying the hypothesis," of discarding hypotheses as unnecessary once the transition to *noesis* has been accomplished. This is what mathematicians fail to do, and consequently they remain on the level of *dianoia*. This is also what Watson fails to do. Mathematics does not rise above hypotheses, but assumes them to be the ultimate intellectual accomplishment. The philosopher, through *noesis*, sees them as hypotheses ("things laid down") by which the mind rises through higher hypotheses to the highest principles, or, according to Plato, the Forms. The mind investigates its own basic principles until it arrives at an unhypothetical starting point. Dialectic tries to discover the philosophical foundations of mathematics, by ascending from hypothesis to find more fundamental principles from which they can be derived.

For Plato, mathematics functions as a preliminary study for philosophy, a systematic training which enables the mind to arrive at the Forms. Pythagorean mathematics indicated a changeless world of ideas that lies beyond or behind the visible world of experience (or, to use Plato's metaphor, outside of the cave). This changeless world imparts order and regularity to the visible world, and makes it more plausible to believe in the changeless Forms of concepts like "equality," "justice" and "beauty." We would not be able to determine whether one action is more just than another, for example, if we did not have a conception of absolute justice as a standard of reference. The Forms are not acquired from observing human behavior—the imperfect does not give knowledge of the perfect. Rather, we recognize that we're already acquainted with them.

"What are the 'Forms?' "

"Correct. We'll also accept 'Ideas'. Nicely done. And now for our Final *Jeopardy!* round." Let's take a look at the category: 'Greek Mythology.' We'll return with the clue, right after this."

Final *Jeopardy!* Tying It All Together

"The Final *Jeopardy!* category is 'Greek Mythology.' Here's the clue: 'Ancient sculptor whose statues were said to be so life-like that they would run away if they were not tied down.' "

Philosophers are not satisfied with accurately stating isolated facts, but try to link their ideas together into a rational framework. Until we connect these truths to other truths that are known and established they remain unexamined opinions. So, how does Socrates suggest we tie our own opinions together into a coherent framework of truth?

In the *Meno*, Socrates mentions a strange belief once held by the Pythagoreans, a cult of religious and philosophical thinkers, that the human soul is capable of recollecting or remembering eternal truths. According to this belief, the soul is immortal and has become acquainted with eternal truths (the Forms) before it enters the body. All learning, then, is a process of remembering or recollecting these unchanging ideas. For Socrates, recollection is a process of working back and examining the content of your mind. Socrates assumes there is a rational relationship between true opinions, but it's up to us to establish that relationship. In doing so, we become aware that all cognition is recognition.

This process of anamnesis, or recollection, allows us to examine the contents of our words, to link our true opinions and beliefs together, and to tie them down. Socrates mentions the statues of Daedalus were so lifelike they needed to be tied down or they would run away. So, too, we can be deceived into believing that a machine like Watson thinks like a human since it is so human-like. Watson is a human creation, like the automatons designed by ancient artists and sculptors that mimicked human behavior. It "thinks" like a human (in terms of *dianoia*), but it can run away (from the truth) because it doesn't know how to determine if it knows anything with any kind of certainty.

Unlike Watson, humans are capable of a direct apprehension of the Forms (the "aha" moment) and we can tie our opinions together by showing that they cohere with other ideas that we know and are established. After they are tied down they become knowledge and remain in place. Anamnesis does this.

Knowledge is therefore prized more highly than true opinion. Moreover, knowledge and, in turn, *noesis*, gives humans a level of understanding and certainty that is not accessible to machines or computers.

"Who is Daedalus?"

"That is the correct answer, and that concludes our Final *Jeopardy!* round."

Is guessing as good as knowing? In *Jeopardy!* the answer is yes. If you guess well, accurately and quickly, you can win the game, even if you don't know *that* you know or *how* you know or *why* you know. But for Plato, knowledge is direct apprehension of the Forms and includes understanding the interrelatedness of ideas. All of this, of course, takes time, and, well, it looks like we're out of time. . . .

"Thank you and please join us again."

I'll Take Twentieth Century, Alex

Here Are the Answers
(For the Questions, see page 187)

(For the Questions, see page 187)

1. This, according to Princeton philosopher Harry Frankfurt, is what results when a speaker has little regard for truth.

2. This famous argument by John Searle implies that your laptop can't understand anything.

3. What you'd deliberate behind if, according to John Rawls, you wished to identify the principles needed to establish a truly just society.

4. Philosopher of science Paul Feyerabend quoted this Cole Porter lyric to describe his theory of epistemological anarchy.

5. According to legend, this tool was used to help settle an argument between Karl Popper and Ludwig Wittgenstein in an unheated Oxford seminar room.

6. This German-born philosopher who died in 1970 promoted the view that many standard philosophical problems are pseudoproblems arising from confused language.

7. This is one game that God does not play, Albert Einstein famously quipped.

8. This feline knows nothing about quantum physics yet made an important contribution to philosophy of science.

9. In 1940 Bishop Manning denounced him as a "man who is a recognized propagandist against both religion and morality, and who specifically defends adultery."

10. Author of *Animal Liberation* and *Practical Ethics*, this philosopher is seen as the champion of animal rights.

11. Losing all vision in his right eye to a disease known as strabismus, this philosopher grew up walleyed.

12. The *Virtue of Selfishness* is a book expressing this philosopher's "objective" view of ethics.

13. Husserl, Heidegger, Sartre, and Merleau-Ponty are all adherents of this school of philosophy.

14. The performance of this ballet in 1913 Paris provoked a riot.

15. The absurdity of life does not mean we should commit suicide, concludes this French writer in a 1942 philosophical essay.

16. This philosopher claimed that we wouldn't want to live inside an "experience machine" that perfectly gave us all the experiences of a good and happy life.

17. This hugely successful 1936 book by A.J. Ayer popularized the philosophical approach known as logical positivism.

18. According to this Austrian philosopher, in a book published in 1934, science does not try to prove, but always tries to disprove, its theories.

19. This philosophical program, drawing on Marx, Engels, and Lenin was once the official philosophy of the Soviet Union.

20. This philosophical program, drawing on Aquinas and Aristotle, was once the official philosophy of the Roman Catholic Church, but was abandoned as such by Pope John Paul II.

21. Upon being asked his opinion of *this* philosophical program, the famously witty Sidney Morgenbesser is said to have replied, "It's all good in theory, but it doesn't work so well in practice."

22. "Society is one word, but many things," wrote this American philosopher and educator.

23. Berggasse 19.

24. This painting by a Norwegian is often said to capture the essence of existential despair.

25. This writer was the first to use the phrase "cold war" to refer to the antagonism between Communism and the West.

26. This American writer translated *Bambi* into English and later accused a high-ranking government official of espionage.

27. According to a logical implication of induction pointed out by this noted philosopher, the existence of one green apple supports the claim that all ravens are black.

28. Approximately 2.71828.

29. This famous twentieth-century philosopher had not one but two unique relationships to Nazism: first as the lover of Martin Heidegger, and then as a reporter at the Jerusalem trial of Adolf Eichmann.

30. Documentary filmmaker Errol Morris has controversially claimed that this philosopher once threw an ashtray at him.

III

You Control
the Board

10
Truth in the Form of a Question

DANIEL WANLESS

As an armchair *Jeopardy!* contestant I love to play along and see how many correct responses I get each episode. In order to do this, I have to blurt out an answer in my living room before the contestant does, so that I am not influenced by their response. So, when I watch *Jeopardy!* at home, I call out a response for every answer, regardless of whether I feel as though I really know it. I have found that I seem to do best when I simply go with the first thing that comes to my mind, even if I am unsure.

When I second-guess my initial thought and come up with something else, I'm more often wrong than right. As a result, I've adopted a policy of going with my first thought when I answer questions while watching the show. In many cases the topic is one I have very little knowledge of and so I am not even quite sure how what pops into my head could be right, but often times it is, because it seems at some point in my life my mind has absorbed some information that correlates a fact in the answer with my response.

So, I know the right response, even though I don't know it. Perhaps you've experienced something similar yourself when playing along at home. The question is, why?

Possibly it's because truths are inside us in a way that we are unaware of. Socrates (around 470–399 B.C.E.) thought so. Socrates is generally considered to be the founder of Western philosophy. The word 'philosophy' in Greek means "love of wisdom." Socrates was the ultimate lover of wisdom in that he questioned everything in order to find the truth. The essence of

Socrates's pursuit of wisdom was his insistence on asking people questions.

Socrates is a difficult figure to make sense of because, similar to Jesus, he never wrote anything in his life, and all the knowledge we have of him comes from the depictions of others, mostly his student Plato. Plato wrote many philosophical dialogues and Socrates was the main character in nearly all of them. Plato was a great philosopher in his own right who often expressed his own philosophical views through the character Socrates; At other times he records biographical facts and philosophical views of the real Socrates.

While it's clear that Plato was inspired and greatly influenced by Socrates, it's far less clear which dialogues represent Socrates's actual ideas as opposed to those of Plato. Scholars generally agree that at least some of the biographical and philosophical content in Plato's work comes from Socrates, especially in Plato's earliest dialogues.

We know Socrates examined life by asking questions. He spent his life questioning everything, from the legitimacy of the political powers of Athens, to the nature of beauty and love. For Socrates, this meant that life was not so much about finding the right answers as it was about asking the right questions.

Similar to Socrates, *Jeopardy!* famously reverses the typical question-answer format. How many times have we heard Alex remind a contestant to respond in the form of a question? The show's inventor, Merv Griffin, explained how this peculiar concept came about while he was having a conversation with his wife: "I was mulling over game show ideas, when she noted that there had not been a successful "question and answer" game on the air since the quiz show scandals. Why not do a switch, and give the answers to the contestant and let them come up with the question? She fired a couple of answers to me: "5,280"—and the question of course was "How many feet in a mile?" Another was "79 Wistful Vista," that was Fibber and Molly McGee's address. I loved the idea, went straight to NBC with the idea, and they bought it without even looking at a pilot show."[1]

---

[1] Cynthia Lowry, "Merv Griffin: Question and Answer Man," *Independent Star-News* (March 29th, 1964). *Fibber McGee and Molly* was a very popular radio show, aired from 1935 to 1959.

The *Jeopardy!* Round: How Do You Know?

Jeopardy! gives answers and forces contestants to produce questions, yet these questions are unlike those of Socrates, for they are questions where the answer has already been provided. Actually, Socrates once argued that in order for people to ask questions at all, the answer would already have to be provided. Plato writes about a now famous discussion Socrates had with a thinker named Meno in which they tried to discover the true nature of virtue. In the course of their discussion, Meno raises one of the most famous conundrums in the history of thought. He says, "And how will you enquire, Socrates, into that which you do not know? What will you put forth as the subject of enquiry? And if you find what you want, how will you ever know that this is the thing which you did not know?" (*Meno*, 80d).

Imagine you're a contestant on *Jeopardy!* and you have control of the board. You select "Famous Philosophers" for $300, confident that you'll do well in this area. The following bewildering text appears on the screen,

Ο φιλόσοφος που έγινε διάσημη του Hegel διαλεκτική στο κεφάλι του.   .

Shockingly, instead of reading the answer, Alex says, "I'll let you figure out what this says."

Can you give the correct response? What if Alex helps out by offering you a list of responses, one of which is correct. Does this help?

Who is René Descartes?

Who is Friedrich Nietzsche?

Who is Aristotle?

Who is Søren Kierkegaard?

Who is Karl Marx?

Which of the above is the correct response? I wrote the answer in Greek, and if you don't know that language, you'll have no idea which of the responses, if any, is correct. The only way for you to ever discover the correct response is for you to actually understand what you are reading (the answer, by the way, is: the famous political philosopher who turned Hegel's dialectic on its head—Karl Marx). Do you see the problem? Because you don't know what an answer says, you cannot pick out the correct response, even when it is staring you in the face. Relatedly, if you do understand the answer properly this means you possess a certain level of knowledge, even if it is only the amount necessary to properly search for the information required to formulate the answer.

What guides the human search for knowledge? How do we know which direction to go if the place we are going is somewhere we have never been?

Meno makes the same point about the search for knowledge in general. If you don't know that you don't know something, how can you ever know that you don't know it? And if you do know something, you know that you know it, which means you don't need to seek it. In other words, how is searching for the truth even possible? If we lack the truth we won't know what we are searching for, and if we know the truth, then we don't need to search for it.

One possible response to this dilemma—known as the Meno Paradox—is to conclude that knowledge is indeed impossible for anyone who searches for it. As Socrates puts it in *Meno* (80d–e), "I know, Meno, what you mean . . . You argue that man cannot enquire either about that which he knows, or about that which he does not know; for if he knows, he has no need to enquire; and if not, he cannot; for he does not know the very subject about which he is to enquire."

Socrates rejects this conclusion and instead solves the problem in a way that is relevant to *Jeopardy!* He tells Meno that the human soul is immortal. For Socrates this means not only that we will live forever in the future, but that we existed for an eternity in the past. According to Socrates, prior to entering into a human body the soul exists in a heavenly world surrounded by undiluted truth. This gives each human soul direct access to absolute knowledge, so that every person enters into this life with the truth already inside of them.

Plato tells us in *Meno* (81a–e)—through Socrates—"The soul, then, as being immortal, and having been born again many times, and having seen all things that exist, whether in this world or in the world below, has knowledge of them all; and it is no wonder that she should be able to call to remembrance all that she ever knew about virtue, and about everything; for as all nature is akin, and the soul has learned all things; there is no difficulty in her eliciting or as men say learning, out of a single recollection—all the rest, if a man is strenuous and does not faint; for all enquiry and all learning is but recollection."

In *Jeopardy!* the reason a contestant can produce the right question is because they already have been given the answer, and the answer given by Alex directs their mental search for the proper question. In the same way, Socrates claims that the only way for someone to pursue the truth through questions is if he already has some sense of what the answer is. The way to find the truth is by remembering it, because it is, in fact, already inside of you, even though you don't realize it.

In this way, Socrates saw himself not as a teacher, or even possessor, of wisdom, but rather as one who could induce others into producing wisdom. In fact, In Plato's *Theaetetus* Socrates compared himself to a midwife, or someone who helped others give birth:

> My art of midwifery is in general like theirs [real midwives]; the only difference is that . . . my concern is not with the body but with the soul that is in travail of birth. And the highest point of my art is the power to prove by every test whether the offspring of a young man's thought is a false phantom or instinct with life and truth. I am so far like the midwife that I cannot myself give birth to wisdom, and the common reproach is true, that, though I question others, I can myself bring nothing to light because there is no wisdom in me. The reason is this. The god constrains me to serve as a midwife, but has debarred me from giving birth. So of myself I have no sort of wisdom, nor has any discovery ever been born to me as the child of my soul. Those who frequent my company at first appear, some of them, quite unintelligent, but, as we go further with our discussions, all who are favored by heaven make progress at a rate that seems surprising to others as well as to themselves, although it is clear that they have never learned anything from me. The many admirable truths they bring to birth have been discovered by themselves from within. But the delivery is heaven's work and mine. (150b–c)

Double *Jeopardy!*: Not Knowing that You Know

During Ken Jennings's historic *Jeopardy!* run he made an appearance on the *Tonight Show* with Jay Leno to discuss his success. Jay observed that oftentimes Ken seemed to buzz in without knowing the correct response. Then, almost miraculously, he would come up with the correct question before he ran out of time. Jay asked Ken, how do you do this? Ken answered that he didn't consciously know the right question when he buzzed in, but that the correct response was somewhere in his unconscious and it somehow popped up in time.

This reminds me of a story concerning a friend of mine, about a time when he was playing a trivia game with his wife. He read to her this question: Who won an acting award for the movie *Lilies of the Field*? She said, "I have no idea, I've never even seen Sidney Poitier."

She meant to say that she had never seen *Lilies of the Field*, but, inexplicably to her, she responded correctly. Even though she wasn't conscious of it, she knew the right answer to the question. Knowledge of the type we have been discussing obviously comes through some experience that we don't remember we had. In fact, Freud modified Socrates's concept of innate knowledge in part by introducing the notion of the subconscious. The point, though, is that the truth is inside of us in some murky way.

In addition to knowledge that is lingering in our subconscious from some past experience, in the *Meno* Socrates argues that innate knowledge is confirmed by the fact that there are certain things we seem able to know without any experience. In philosophical terms, this is referred to as *a priori* knowledge—*a priori* is Latin for "before experience."

Jeopardy! also involves knowledge that is generated in a more logical manner. Recently, Watson—a super-computer developed by IBM—demonstrated the development of artificial intelligence by handily defeating two *Jeopardy!* champions. A super-computer has access to information that the human mind cannot compete with, yet the gap between these machines and human beings has never been the possession of knowledge itself but its synthesis. Think of a *Jeopardy!* category that names three places and the goal is to name which one is southernmost. For Example:

Des Moines

Saint Louis

Omaha

This specific answer is the type of thing that no particular person has ever considered until faced with it. How is it solved? By taking a bunch of knowledge about different places and synthesizing it, and generating the logical response based on the data.

The reason a human can generate a correct response to this type of puzzle is that humans come equipped with the logical abilities necessary to analyze the answer in the right way. Logic seems to be primarily what Socrates means when he suggests that the truth is already on the inside of us. Logic gives us the ability to do math and everything that entails, but it also gives us the ability to take new information and distinguish what is true from what is false based on the law of non-contradiction. If we know that Saint Louis is south of Omaha, and we know that Omaha is south of Des Moines, then we can conclude using logic alone that Saint Louis must be south of Des Moines, for otherwise the world would be contradictory. This seeming innate ability to apply logic to any issue is part of the crux of Socrates's notion of innate, partial knowledge, that, when applied correctly to the world around us can lead us to new, previously unknown conclusions.

In the *Meno* Socrates proved this phenomena himself by taking a slave boy and asking him questions about the mathematical dimensions of side of a square with twice the area of the square.

Tell me, boy, is not
this a square of four
feet which I have drawn
(Plato, Meno, 82b)?

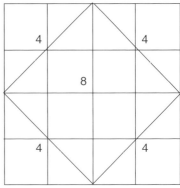

The boy had never been educated in mathematics and at first claims ignorance about the answer. But Socrates continues to question the boy until he actually produces the right answer to the question. Socrates concludes that the right answer was always inside of the boy in the form of pure logical and mathematical concepts, and asking him the right questions allowed him to recognize the latent truth inside of him.

Final *Jeopardy!* Knowing that You Don't Know

In *Final Jeopardy!* contestants are given a category and must then use their existing money to make a wager about their providing the correct "answer" before knowing what the "question" is. One of the factors they must consider is the level of knowledge they have about the particular category. The difference between winning and losing comes down to whether they make the right wager, but how can you make an accurate wager when you don't know what the answer is?

Imagine the final category is Romance Films. You may know almost everything there is to know about romance movies, because you have seen and studied almost all of them . . . except for *The Notebook*. What if the answer is from that movie?

Statisticians have discussed the issues involved in making the best bet possible during *Final Jeopardy!* However, when it comes to wagering, the only irrefutable fact in *Final Jeopardy!* is that you don't know whether or not you know the right response. In light of this fact, how should you play? Using statistical analysis can limit the degree of error somewhat, but the great unquantifiable unknown is what the actual answer will be, for no matter how much you know about a given subject, the vast amount that you do not know is typically far greater.

Go with Your Gut

As I said, going with your gut in *Jeopardy!* often produces better results than carefully deliberating about the answer. Part of the problem with *Final Jeopardy!* is that contestants have more time to second-guess their instincts. Nothing is worse than seeing a contestant in *Final Jeopardy!* who wrote out the right response before crossing it out and putting something else down. Going too far north eventually takes us south, and too much thinking can get us the same result as not thinking at all.

The dilemma posed in *Final Jeopardy!* is similar to the dilemma posed in real life. Each day every person is forced to make decisions based on limited information. The consequences of any decision can be enormous. Should I take this job? Is Steve the one I should marry? Søren Kierkegaard, a devotee of Socrates, wrote in his journals (IV A 164): "Life is only understood backwards, but it must be lived forwards." Given this reality, what if I ask you, how should you live your life? What is the best way to live?

Socrates's inverse of the question-answer format provided him with a notion of the best way to live one's life. He believed that a life of posing questions was superior to a life of providing pat answers. He believed this so strongly that he devoted his life to questioning citizens on the streets of Athens about the nature of love, truth, and beauty. This landed him in court, where he was charged with blasphemy and corrupting the youth of Athens. Socrates opted to defend himself, and according to Plato's *Apology* (38a), at his trial he uttered the now famous words, "The unexamined life is not worth living." What he meant was that a life in which he didn't continually question things would be pointless, for wisdom was found in getting better at asking questions.

Perhaps the best way to sum up Socrates's point is this: The truth is that humans really don't know things in the way we would like, or often presume to know. This means we must cling to questions, not answers. However, the questions that we formulate often seem to indicate that we really do have the answers buried deep in our souls. So, we do know that we don't really know, but this means that we do know something after all.

Socrates answered the ultimate question by saying that a life of questioning is the best and most worthwhile way to live life. In a sense, Socrates saw that the right answer was wrapped up in the question itself, for the only real fact that human beings can operate from is their ignorance. What we know for certain, just like contestants at the beginning of Final *Jeopardy!*, is that we don't know for certain. Since we don't know for certain, we ought to spend our lives embracing that uncertainty by producing questions rather than answers.

Socrates was so certain of that conclusion that he said at his trial that if he were convicted of the charges and given the option of being set free on the condition that he no longer question things, he would have to refuse and instead choose death, for if he were to continue living he would have to continue questioning.

What Would Socrates Do? Bet It All

I suppose we can't be certain about how Socrates would wager in *Final Jeopardy!*, but given what we know about him, it seems reasonable to think that he would go all in. This is because in real life he valued courage and bet it all on the idea that questioning everything was the right way to live.

Socrates could have hedged his bets, he could have thought about the real possibility that he was wrong and that questioning everything was not the right way to live one's life. He could have made a deal to discontinue his way of life in order to preserve his own existence. After all, perhaps he was wrong, and if he continued to live he could discover his error over time and acquire the truth. He could have, but he didn't.

Socrates could have saved his life by altering his action, but to do so would be to alter the core conviction that made him who he was, and in the end that would be no existence at all, for he would live on only by losing his very self.

Consequently, Socrates would bet everything on his knowledge of the right way to live because he had studied life to such a degree that his knowledge was on the inside of him, a part of who he was. If it turned out that he was wrong on the final question, he would lose, but he would lose being courageous, and that would be better than winning but having no courage at all.

Fighting Words

Perhaps surprisingly, the idea that true knowledge is already inside of us was not something Socrates believed beyond question. After all, though there are reasons to think innate knowledge might be right, as we have seen, there are also reasons to be skeptical about any conclusion we might have. In fact, it seems Socrates's student Plato was more convinced of it than was Socrates. Nevertheless, Socrates's uncertainty about his human circumstances and the exact nature of human knowledge didn't make him waffle in his belief about the necessity of questioning, but rather gave him resolution.

Concerning the idea of innate knowledge, in Plato's *Meno* (86b) he said "Most of the points I have made in my argument are not such as I would fight for. But the belief that we shall be better and braver and less helpless if we think that we ought to inquire, than we should have been if we thought that there was no knowing and no duty to seek to know what we do not know;—that is a belief for which I am ready to fight, in word and deed, to the utmost of my power." Socrates's belief in innate knowledge was based more on an ethical concern than philosophical certainty. If you live the way Socrates did you can be confident at life's ultimate trials because you know you have lived the right way and you know yourself thoroughly.

A lifetime of accumulating knowledge is required to have any shot at being successful on *Jeopardy!* In *Final Jeopardy!* each contestant has to have confidence that the years of preparation will give them a good shot at responding correctly. Xenophon recounts in his work, *The Defense of Socrates,* that when Socrates was facing charges that could result in his own execution, people were surprised because he seemed to be putting no time at all into preparing a defense for himself. When someone asked him about this, Socrates replied that he didn't need to do so, because had been preparing for this trial his entire life.

Indeed, his entire life was a preparation for this final moment of jeopardy, for he believed his life in the form of a question was the true response to the answer, "the best way to live one's life", and its form was just as Alex would have it.

11
It's Been an Education

MATT KOHLSTEDT

Being a contestant on *Jeopardy!* is what psychologist-philosopher Abraham Maslow called a "peak experience." Characteristics of a peak experience include losing track of time, being at one with the universe, and feeling separate from one's body. Check that: *winning* on *Jeopardy!* is a peak experience. Losing stinks. At least that was the case for me. In one day of taping, I won five games. I was not uniformly brilliant in each performance, and two of my victories involved a good deal of luck. But when I look back on that Wednesday in Culver City, I know that my best moments were when I didn't think about the cameras, viewers, or competitors, and just let the experience flow.

According to Maslow, peak experiences don't last long. They are exultant moments rather than sustained periods of elation or transcendence. My own *Jeopardy!* high was cut short by the sudden illness and death of my grandpa. He got sick in November, shortly after my winning streak in Culver City. When I left the Tournament of Champions in January, it was to go to his funeral. None of my shows had even aired yet.

As a result, I found myself trapped in a bizarre television purgatory. Something had happened to me in November, but, since I never told my grandpa about it, it was somehow less real when the shows actually aired in January and March. It felt as though the time-space continuum had somehow ruptured. When I tried out for the show, I imagined it as a tribute to the value that my grandpa placed on education. I thought that a public display of his grandson's knowledge would be something for him to look forward to, to brag about, to have some fun with. Instead, I was left with the heartache of losing my grandfather, while also mourning my own rotten performance at the Tournament of Champions.

It was through this extended grieving process that I began to think that my grandpa might not have cared very much that I had won a game show. He would have been interested, and proud, but he probably wouldn't have seen it as a culmination of a lifetime of formal education, or a tribute to his career as a professor of education, or really, as having anything to do with knowledge as he saw it. I came to this realization after reading my grandpa's book on teacher education. In that book, he applied Maslow's theory of self-actualization to the process of teacher training. It brought me to see a side of my grandpa I had never known. It made me understand the role that *Jeopardy!* played in my own life, and the way in which *Jeopardy!* can guide us to a useful Philosophy of Education for today.

The *Jeopardy!* Effect and High-Stakes Testing

Victory on *Jeopardy!* is only partly attributable to education or knowledge. The smartest contestant doesn't always win. Indeed, *Jeopardy!* would never have attracted a loyal, passionate, and dynamic fan base if the results were so simple or predictable. Instead, there's a magic alchemy of gamesmanship, showmanship, and knowingship that go into making a great *Jeopardy!* contestant. If the smartest or most educated person won every time, there would be no suspense. As sports commentators like to say, that's why they play the games.

So, while no *Jeopardy!* viewers are likely to confuse success on *Jeopardy!* with pure intellect, in the debate over standardized testing in schools we have what might be called the *Jeopardy!*-ization of schooling. (It works out well for my purposes here that I think the undue emphasis of testing in schools is placing students in jeopardy, but I would make this argument even if the show were called *Safety!*) Some people might think that school would be awesome if it were more like *Jeopardy!* They would be right, if every classroom had writing staff to craft fascinating questions full of clever wordplay. Unfortunately, wordplay is not the basis of an educational system. In fact, there's not much play of any kind in most class-rooms today. And that is not a good thing.

Playing *Jeopardy!* as an in-class review before tests is a time-tested favorite of both students and teachers, but should not be mistaken for a form of teaching. For both teachers and students, testing has taken over the classroom experience. Teachers often feel anxious if they deviate from the curriculum. The test scores of students are linked to teachers' performance reviews, which, in turn, can determine their employment status. Teachers without tenure can be fired if their students' test scores don't reach the level where statisticians determine they should be. Some school districts have started to experiment with paying teachers more for raising their students' test scores. This represents a positive incentive, unlike the negative incentive of being fired, but it still leads us to the same place: more emphasis on testing.

I don't think that students shouldn't be tested. Tests are highly motivating. I personally enjoy taking tests. I usually do well on them. Doing well on tests probably correlates with doing well on *Jeopardy!*, but *Jeopardy!* is a game show, not a basis for an educational system.

My concern is that discourse today about education is more functional than philosophical. Most commentators agree that something must be done to fix the "broken" educational system. However, the maturity of the US educational system leads us to take some of the system's basic qualities for granted, as though the system itself is a crotchety old person, too set in his ways to change. Reformers need to examine more closely the role that education will play in twenty-first century America before they seek to graft additional layers of complexity onto an already complicated system. We need a philosophy of education that also includes a philosophy of educators. In other words, we need to look more closely at the role educators are meant to fill in society.

Today what we hear about teachers is that they are either good or bad. Good teachers move their students along at an above-average rate. Bad teachers are those who do not even advance their students a full grade level over the course of a school year. These are the baseline assumptions. In this model, teachers are assembly-line workers filling students with standardized information, and the students are trained to regurgitate the information at the right time. The only people who benefit from this test-first arrangement are the manufacturers of number two pencils. Can we get those people before a congressional subcommittee? I'd like to know who Faber and Castell are, anyway.

One of the things I learned from being on *Jeopardy!* is the way in which the spotlight affects performance. I buzzed in on questions I knew, and when Alex said 'Matt', it was as though I had been hypnotized to lose all cognitive function.'[1] I gave the wrong answers to things I had studied, like the number of articles in the US Constitution. This is what I call the *Jeopardy!* effect, and it's real. Before I was on the show, I used to yell at contestants when they would miss something I thought was obvious. Now I just shake my head and remember, "*Jeopardy!* viewers think I think there are only five articles in the Constitution, when I swear I know there are seven."

The *Jeopardy!* effect is similar to the test effect that students experience when taking high-stakes exams. They can forget everything they learned in one bad morning. Or they can have a cold. Or they might not care. Or they may be burnt out from answering practice test questions every day of the school year, as some students are asked to do, and are then incapable of mustering the effort to do well on the test, regardless of how exercised their teacher is over the whole thing. The point is that standardized tests are imprecise measures of imperfect creatures within inconsistent conditions. We do not take the measure of individuals based on their performance on *Jeopardy!* And I certainly don't blame other people for my own poor performance. Yet it seems to me as if teachers are being held fully accountable for test scores that are only partially within their control.

It's not that teachers should be asked to do less. They need to be allowed to do more. Teachers are most able to inspire, motivate, transform when they are given time and space to identify and cultivate the talents and aptitudes within individual children. For my money, the most important thing that a teacher can impart to a student is an ability and eagerness to

---

[1] As Dan Melia points out in this volume, the folks at *Jeopardy!* insist on referring to the buzzer as a "signaling device," but if I say "I signaled in" it sounds like I was waving a nautical flag instead of pressing a button.

independently learn new things. But in order to nurture that ability, teachers need to know their students as more than just empty vessels to be filled with information.

How Maslow Can We Go?

Unlike in *Jeopardy!*, not all problems in life have readily available answers. This banal statement should identify for us the problem with making school a repository for endless questioning and answering. (Or answering and questioning, as the case may be.) As a society, we take the fun out of learning, and rob students of an opportunity to figure out how to learn for themselves.

Philosophy as a mode of thought can help ascribe meaning to the functioning of society that we might otherwise take for granted. Debates over philosophy are ways of deciding what is at stake. In the case of philosophy of education, we should be thinking about what purpose education serves in society. Articulating a philosophy of education should be the first step of any reform process. Some educational reformers seem to want to get to the next step without first examining the reasons it's worth getting there.

People of both Maslow's and my grandpa's generations must have been stunned by the rapidity of human progress. Whereas human existence had previously been highly contingent on health and resources, in the twentieth century, illnesses were inoculated against, and farms became more efficient. Scarcity, which had been the defining state of existence, was seemingly on the verge of being eliminated. It made sense to think about how education should be different if the products of that educational system were going to be leading radically different lives than the generations prior to them. Maslow considered self-actualization to be a worthy goal of a society that could take care of its citizens' basic needs.

That kind of philosophical thinking is largely absent from discussions of educational reform today. In fact, it was largely peripheral to many of the discussions that have occurred previously. But that doesn't mean we can't reintroduce it now.

In order to think philosophically about education, readers need only reflect on what they found most valuable in their own educations. Most likely, it had nothing to do with a formal piece of curriculum. My guess is that the moment (or moments) that stand out in most peoples' minds are the ones in which a teacher expressed an interest in them. Not as a statistic to boost, or as a means of getting paid more, but as a human whose development mattered. Teachers today are in danger of losing that opportunity. With increased pressure to deliver results, they are inevitably passing some of that pressure down to their students, and losing any personal touch in the process.

In *Jeopardy!* terms, a teacher taking an interest in a student outside of the class's content is akin to the mid-round interview. To some people, the interview with Alex is merely an awkward intermission that distracts from the game play. But I think that the interview is precisely what makes the show's appeal endure. I went through a period of watching *Jeopardy!* when I would fast forward through the interviews. I stopped enjoying the show, because I stopped caring about the participants. Without a brief exposure to the contestants' personalities, the viewing experience truly became a sequence of decontextualized information. The same thing can occur in the classroom if teachers can't deviate from the curriculum.

It turns out my grandpa already viewed teacher education in this somewhat unorthodox way. Before I left town after my grandpa's funeral, I grabbed a copy of the book he co-authored in 1975, *A Partnership for the Supervision of Student Teachers*. It had been sitting on a shelf in his guest bedroom for my entire life. My grandpa was in charge of the student teacher program at Indiana University. His job was to place student teachers in classrooms around the state. I always assumed that his job was pretty straightforward. I had gone to a couple of the meetings of the professional organization he belonged to, but by that time he had retired, and was more accustomed to meeting old friends in the bar than he was to discussing and examining pertinent issues in his field.

What I read in the book surprised me. What stood out in particular was a chapter in which he applied Maslow's theory of motivation to the context of supervising student teachers. Here was my grandpa, talking about the ways in which teacher educators could help student teachers to become self-actualized. He wrote:

> ... the type of product that teacher educators hope to produce is a beginning teacher who enjoys working with pupils, finds great satisfaction in helping them learn; who possesses the necessary skills to accomplish this end; and who is open to new ideas and experiences so that she can grow in the teaching profession.
>
> This goal is virtually identical with a construct that Abraham Maslow calls the *self-actualized* person, operating in a synergic environment. Maslow's self-actualized person is realizing his or her fullest potential, becoming the best that he or she can become. By a synergic environment, Maslow means an environment in which the needs of the individual and the needs of those with whom he or she associates are together satisfied by the mutual relationship.
>
> According to Maslow almost everyone is born with a *need* for self-actualization, an instinctive desire to become the best that one can become. But one is also born with *other* needs that are stronger than the need for self-actualization, and that these must be gratified before one is even concerned about becoming self-actualized. These more powerful needs are: physiological; safety; love and belongingness; and esteem.

Some of the passages in this book were borderline New Age philosophy. Just reconciling my image of my grandpa with his book's content has taken some time. As far as I could tell, my grandpa's sense of self-actualization involved Budweiser and a pig roast. What was this talk of a "synergic environment"? I wasn't sure that my grandpa would recognize synergy without the help of powerful narcotics that were beyond his pay grade.

The more I learned about Maslow's theory of education, though, the more I understood that Maslow (and my grandpa) were, some forty to fifty years ago, talking about teachers in a way that is completely unfamiliar to the way people talk today. Today's teachers must prepare students for a battery of tests that not only dictates what can be taught, but also determines their very career paths. (A group of tests is called a battery because they leave the takers beaten up and drained of energy.) With the recent introduction of free market principles such as performance pay, not to mention actions such as the release of student test scores, teachers are under increasing external pressures. It should not be surprising that national surveys report teacher morale to be at all-time lows.

Teaching has always been a difficult job. It has never been particularly well paid. (And *Jeopardy!*'s new teacher tournament can only do so much to remedy that shortcoming.) Nevertheless, many teachers put in days that go well beyond their classroom time in order to provide the best possible learning environment for their students. Teaching as a profession has always had a high rate of attrition, and it is increasing. We also know that top students rarely choose teaching as a top-choice career.

There are strong and articulate advocates who are mounting powerful defenses for the teaching profession. I have found, though, that educational reform is still often couched in terms that minimize teachers. I'm not even referring to the blatant propaganda that talks about how easy teaching is, and how teaching is a fallback profession for those people who can't do anything in the real world. Most reasonable people agree that teaching is an indispensable, noble profession. But even among those who want to reform the teaching profession, all the talk is of servicing students.

Maslow's theory of education instead focuses on helping teachers become self-actualized in order to become better educators. In other words, it prioritizes the personal and professional development of educators. To be clear, Maslow contended that teachers who were self-actualized would be better teachers for their students. In the end, students would still be the beneficiaries. But he believed that the educational system as a whole would be enhanced through advocating for teacher self-actualization.

The Values Worth Adding

In addition to imparting content, teachers are also supposed to impart life skills and career motivation. That, at least, is the contention of the value-added movement, which has sought to track children from grade school through their professional career. The value-added movement has been responsible for spreading the idea that "good" teachers can add millions of dollars to the economy over the course of their careers, due to the additional earning capacity of their students. That such an idea has gained any traction should be our greatest indication that Americans need to learn more practical math and logic skills.

By this perverse ranking system, the teacher who happened to teach the most bankers, or one successful internet entrepreneur, becomes the model on which future teachers should be trained. To be sure, there are many important jobs that are well compensated, but the value-added movement equates teachers' values with their students' future earned incomes. We do not need teachers to start telling their students to become lawyers, hedge-fund managers, or highly specialized doctors. Or even multi-million dollar *Jeopardy!* champions, for that matter. We have quite enough people choosing those careers already.

We do need teachers, though, who are able to communicate an ethos. This is where the value-added movement gets really confusing. In addition to ranking teachers according to the cumulative incomes of their former students, the value-added advocates also like to point out that students who have had "good" teachers are more likely to finish high school, as well as less likely to become pregnant during their teenage years. However, neither of these particular outcomes is related to any curriculum that is currently taught in any public school in the United States. There is no English teacher who has a lesson plan about safe sex. Moreover, the student who does not become pregnant as a teenager has not learned that lesson from a teacher. Or, if she has, she has learned it indirectly, through the teacher's emphasis on self-respect, self-control, or some other virtue or value.

Thinking about these attempted reforms philosophically, we begin to see a system that is, to an extent, at war with itself. On the one hand, linking teacher success to their students' future salaries seems to encourage teachers to assign Ayn Rand and urge their students to maximize their earning potential. This logic would demand a system that was based on the most efficient transfer of information from teacher to student, and would indeed lend itself to statistical tracking over time. By the logic of maximizing profit, the best teacher is the one that transfers the most knowledge to the most students.

On the other hand, though, teachers are supposed to add value to society by teaching their students to finish school and not get pregnant. That type of outcome seems to be linked far more to a teacher who would communicate a philosophy of life, or an ethos, or who would simply advocate personal fulfillment over financial enrichment.

Jeopardy! is an analog of the first educational system. People are rewarded for knowing. But no one would ever confuse a successful *Jeopardy!* contestant with an innately good person. In my experience, there are many fine people who become *Jeopardy!* contestants, but their fineness is not in any way linked to their ability to press a button and answer a question. That process is the result more of Pavlovian conditioning in the American educational system than from any desirable personality traits they have picked up over their lifetimes.

I'm all for teachers being given the chance to communicate an ethos. Maslow's philosophy of education is a good place to start. People who are self-actualized can't become self-actualized without understanding their relationships with other people. A person who is self-actualized is not selfish. That person may understand himself or herself more fully, but that understanding is meaningless if it's not in relation to others. With a focus on producing teachers who are liberated to get something out their work, we stand a much better chance of producing teachers who are willing to put everything into their work.

For the Love of Learning

Any success I had on *Jeopardy!* was not a result of knowledge *per se*, but rather of a deeply-held love of learning. I studied before my appearance. It was fun. I re-learned facts I once knew but had forgotten. When I got the call, I adjusted my schedule. I kept teaching my writing course and studying for my comprehensive exams for the ten to twelve hours per day that was typical of my routine at that time.

It would have been nice if the texts I was reading for my comprehensive exams were helpful for *Jeopardy!* purposes, but unfortunately, most history texts today are pretty esoteric, and too specialized to be of use on *Jeopardy!* People have the mistaken impression that grad school is a great time to be on *Jeopardy!* Better to have a nine-to-five job, I think. Have you ever seen a category called "Obscure Mid-Century Activists"?

After working out and eating dinner, I would compete against the television contestants while my wife kept score. Then I would study fact books until midnight or so. I describe these routines not because they were extraordinary. Most contestants have lives outside trivia, I imagine. Nevertheless, they try to squeeze in opportunities to study whenever they can. The point is that my routine became an all-encompassing pursuit.

It was also rather delightful. After two and a half years of graduate study in a program where most people believed that history and identity were contingent and constructed, studying for *Jeopardy!* was a welcome relief. Here were answers! History was not an amalgam of arguments and interventions, but a collection of facts, dates, names, and places! I was able to revert to the question-answer reward system that had been the hallmark of my education to that point. *Jeopardy!* provided a distinctly American analogy for education, in which answers are in fact a means to an end, rather than a mode of developing historical thought or understanding. As right answers became more rare in my graduate study, I was able to seek refuge in the potential of actually being monetarily rewarded for knowing a fact. It was the exact opposite of graduate education in American Studies, where there are no facts, and where there is certainly no money.

The experience of studying for *Jeopardy!* also tuned me in to one of the other disadvantages of increased testing for students: correct answers are intoxicating. At times I felt like a recovering know-it-all having a trivia relapse. I thought those all-night quiz benders were behind me, but "Jeop Prep" brought out the old addict in me.

Just as preparing to be on *Jeopardy!* only prepares a person to be on a quiz show, high-stakes test prep only readies students to take tests. Students brought up on testing seem very likely to long for that type of certitude in the rest of their lives. There is an addictive feeling to accumulating facts and having them at near-instant command. Better instead to cultivate in students some frustration tolerance.

What I am proud of is that my *Jeopardy!* appearances reflected a diligent approach to a problem. I set a goal for myself: that I would try to minimize the number of times on the show that I thought, "Ooh, I knew that . . . once . . ." I focused on studying items that were familiar but not hardwired into my brain. What allowed me to do all that, though, was having had teachers and family members who had cultivated in me an ability to work on a project without immediate reward.

I had a teacher tell me once that she thought I was always in fourth gear, and that if I ever figured out how to shift into fifth gear I could really accomplish something great. After I did well on *Jeopardy!*, I felt as though I had shifted into fifth gear. I had reason to be proud. I decided that my grandpa would have been proud too.

12
Democracy's in *Jeopardy!*

JOSEPH J. FOY

The category: Politics. Your clue: This helps make better citizens through a command of facts and a better understanding of the world. The question: What is *Jeopardy!*?

Though it may seem as though there is little more than a periodic and superficial connection between the popular television game show and notions of citizenship and civics (after all, there are often "politics" and "history" categories sprinkled into each broadcast), *Jeopardy!* at its core reflects important aspects of democracy and what it means to be a citizen in the most profound sense. By testing contestants on a wide variety of topics and subjects, it enables a diversity of talents and proficiencies to shine at different moments and forces its champions to be well-rounded in their knowledge of the world.

Moreover, the competitive and engaging format of the show is one in which knowledge and information are elevated to a position of importance. Audiences are not only able to "play along" and learn with the show, they are also constructing a form of personal identity in which knowledge—so crucial within democratic society—is both valued and rewarded. Ultimately, a show like *Jeopardy!* serves an important social function that cannot be readily dismissed as mere entertainment.

Select a Category

To be a successful *Jeopardy!* contestant, you must possess a wide range of knowledge across a host of subjects. Categories might range from the more obviously political ("government" and "history") to those that are more deeply rooted in a knowledge of culture and a sense of worldly affairs (popular culture, literature, geography, economics, biography, sports, science, or the arts). In a single round a contestant may be asked to name notable characters in literary history, identify geographic locations around the world, be familiar with important scientific contributions, and signify the connection between Archibald Leach, Bernard Schwartz and Lucille LeSueur (sorry, Cliff Clavin, the answer is not, "Who are three people who've never been in my kitchen?"). The diversity of categories is such that no single area of expertise can guarantee a person victory, creating a great leveling effect in terms of knowledge and information.

The variety of knowledge a contestant needs to successfully navigate a round of *Jeopardy!* is not at all far removed from the diverse base of information required to be a fully functioning citizen of a democratic state. Democracy is rooted in the idea that every individual is capable of engaging in a public deliberation of affairs. Likewise, every individual ought to be afforded the same right to help make decisions, in the hope that the deliberative process and aggregation of decisions will yield outcomes that are in the interests of all. Power, in such a system, is horizontally distributed across the whole of society. Citizens in a democracy are, therefore, asked to be at least familiar with a wide range of issues in a host of different areas ranging from political, social, cultural, economic, scientific, historical, and international in nature. To that extent, there is an inherently democratic element to the popular quiz show that requires fluency in all of those areas (and more), which may in part help to explain its continued popularity and success.

Political theorists have long suggested the need for an informed citizenry in order to produce a properly functioning democracy. At a most basic level, citizens need to understand the basic rules that create the framework for engaging in struggles for leadership, as well as the different institutions that comprise the government responsible for making and enforcing decisions that are binding on the population. For citizens to be able to effectively navigate their way through such a political system they must possess a working knowledge of institutions, actors, and processes. As theorists Richard Niemi and Jane June once noted, "democratic citizens should have a minimum understanding of the political system in which they express preferences and elect representatives."[1] This enables citizens to access the system and work toward influencing its actions and outcomes.

However, apart from merely being able to identify and understand how the system works, each individual is being asked to make a rational decision about countless complex issues and outcomes that may arise. In some respects, the only way to prepare effectively for the innumerable questions that confront modern democratic societies is the same way we might prepare for a round of *Jeopardy!*—read, study, and learn as much as you can in order to acquire as much knowledge as possible. Just as in the political realm, there are some subjects and topics that may occur more frequently than others, but the brilliant thing about *Jeopardy!* is that the possibilities are as vast as the frontiers of all human knowledge.

Having at least a working knowledge of many different spheres of information helps to prevent a contestant from feeling overwhelmed by possibility, just like having a well-rounded education about the world helps prevent citizens from feeling as though the political system is just too complicated for them to engage. Therefore, the skills that serve someone well in *Jeopardy!* are the same that will serve individuals well as they participate in democratic society.

There is, of course, the concern that asking people to have competency in so many different areas will lead to a "jack-of-all-trades" mentality that prevents anyone from really flourishing in a single area of expertise. Such criticisms have been leveled at democracy for some time. In his classic work *Democracy in America*, French sociologist Alexis de Tocqueville provided a summary critique of the state of intellectualism in the United States in the mid-1800s. Tocqueville writes:

> It must be acknowledged that in few of the civilized nations of our time have the higher sciences made less progress than in the United States; and in few have great artists, distinguished poets, or celebrated writers, been more rare. (Mentor, 1956, p. 158)

---

[1] Richard Niemi and Jane Junn, *Civic Education; What Makes Students Learn*, Yale University Press, 1998, p. 1.

Laying the blame on the nation's Puritanical origins, its citizens' commercial habits, and the expansive environment in which they lived, Tocqueville argued that the people of the United States have a great command of practical sciences and information, but not the visionary speculation of theory that leads to new breakthroughs and innovations.

In spite of Tocqueville's criticisms, the contributions of American society to the progress of science and technology, as well as the arts and humanities, are well documented in history. American innovators helped to bring about such revolutionary products as the telephone, the airplane, assembly-line production, and the iPod and its numerous variations. Watching a few episodes of *Jeopardy!* will provide even more examples than I can list here, not to mention that it was an American television host and media mogul, Merv Griffin, who created the popular quiz show in 1964.

However, Tocqueville's larger concern about the great middling standard of democratic equality, especially in a heavily commercial republic like that of the United States, is something that is echoed in the writings of many other philosophers writing on the subject of democracy. In *The Republic*, Plato had argued that ordinary people are incapable of self-governance because they do not know how to properly run a state. He suggests that ordinary citizens are simply not familiar enough with such things as economics, military strategy, conditions in other countries, or the complex intricacies of law and ethics to make proper decisions. Plato expressed skepticism that the common citizen would even seek to have a proper understanding of these things. He warns that turning control of the state over to the average person will ultimately end in disaster, just as Tocqueville expressed concern that democracy could lead to tyranny of thought and a preoccupation with consumption and escapism.

What *Jeopardy!* helps reveal is that a person can be both an "expert" in terms of the occupational identity they hold, while at the same time contributing as a "citizen." A deep knowledge and proficiency within a particular field does not preclude someone from also developing a well-rounded knowledge of a variety of subject areas. With many contestants coming from professional, service, and labor backgrounds (Chuck Forrest was a law student, Mark Lowenthal was an educator, Lt. Frank

Spangenberg was a member of the Transit Bureau of the New York City Police Department, and Ken Jennings was a software engineer), as well as individuals who are not in the workforce, *Jeopardy!* illustrates the fact that your profession or expertise need not define or limit you in terms of a robust knowledge of the world.

A Trivial Pursuit?

You might assume that I'm overstating the link between the "trivial" knowledge called for in *Jeopardy!* and the kind of knowledge required for vibrant participation in a democracy. Of course, the creators and producers of the show are not attempting to instill civic virtues in their audiences, nor is the show intended to strengthen the foundations of popular sovereignty. While it is most certainly the case that *Jeopardy!* is not intended as an exercise in democracy, there is a link between democratic citizenship and the kind of information tested on the show.

Rather than merely being an exercise in "recalling information," *Jeopardy!* requires that individuals possess complex language and problem-solving skills, while at the same time having a robust knowledge base for the development of quick analysis and application of information.[2] A recent article in *The Yale Law Journal* argues that the very skills that helped make IBM's Watson a resounding success at *Jeopardy!* could also be translated into helping textualists interpret the law and the Constitution.[3]

Whether Watson could serve as the next Chief Justice of the US Supreme Court, and issues of life-time tenure standards for computers notwithstanding, the knowledge that *Jeopardy!* tests is valuable for better understanding the link between knowledge and democratic citizenship. For instance, *Jeopardy!* often challenges contestants to show their knowledge of the

---

[2] David Ferrucci, et al., "Building Watson: An Overview of the DeepQA Project," *AI Magazine*, Fall 2010,
   <http://www.stanford.edu/class/cs124/AIMagzine-DeepQA.pdf>.

[3] Betsy Cooper, "Judges in Jeopardy!: Could IBM's Watson Beat Courts at Their Own Game?" *Yale Law Journal Online*, <http://yalelawjournal.org/the-yale-law-journal-pocket-part/legislation/judges-in-jeopardy!:-could-ibm%E2%80%99s- watson-beat-courts-at-their-own-game?/>.

Constitution. Here, there is a clear correlation between civic knowledge (understanding facts and information about the state and politics) and *Jeopardy!*.

There are also established correlations between such knowledge and a substantive defense of the principles of democracy. The McCormick Tribune Freedom Museum, for example, found that the less people knew about their rights, even seemingly trivial knowledge like being able to list the five freedoms guaranteed by the First Amendment (religion, speech, press, assembly, and petition), the more willing they were to have those rights stripped away without putting up any kind of defense.[4] Their findings echo the sentiments of the second President of the United States, John Adams, who wrote in "A Dissertation on the Canon and Feudal Law" in 1765 that "liberty cannot be preserved without general knowledge among the people."

The link between knowledge tested on *Jeopardy!* and citizenship, however, extends beyond a working knowledge of politics. Even the most casual viewer of *Jeopardy!* can attest that the categories of information that contestants will be tested on go well beyond issues pertaining to government. You might just as easily need to identify the contributions of Chinese-American architect I.M. Pei as those of constitutional architects like James Madison or Alexander Hamilton. But it's here that *Jeopardy!* provides an even deeper perspective on knowledge and the citizen.

A democracy requires that people be engaged in an ongoing social and cultural discussion about values and traditions and the world around them. It's not enough to merely possess a procedural, or even deep, knowledge about the political system. You must also be able to participate in the broader conversations of the community to truly be a part of the democratic public. Therefore, knowledge that helps an individual navigate through a diversity of subjects in a round of *Jeopardy!* also helps to connect them to the body of knowledge that encompasses the larger public, allowing them to take part in the cultural dialogues that connect people to one another.

The connection between knowledge and engagement also extends beyond the link between knowledge of the political sys-

---

[4] McCormick Tribune Freedom Museum, "Americans' Awareness of First Amendment Freedoms," <http://www.forumforeducation.org/node/147>.

tem and citizen involvement. In fact, one of the strongest predictors of civic engagement and participation within democracy in a variety of forms is the level of a person's educational attainment. The more educated an individual, regardless of their field of study or range of courses, the more likely they are to vote and participate in other forms of political action like contacting elected officials, working in campaigns, attending rallies, and communicating with others about political issues.[5]

This is not to say that education is the sole predictor of a person's knowledge of the world. Brad Rutter, the biggest all-time money winner on the show to-date, dropped out of Johns Hopkins University where he was studying English. However, education does help to broaden a person's understanding of the world around them, and is a good indicator of a wide variety of knowledge skills necessary for navigating democratic society.

Citizens' knowledge not only affects their behavior, it also impacts the operations of government. Political scientists Michael Delli Carpini and Scott Keeter, who extensively analyze the relationship between citizen knowledge and a host of democratic benefits, find that increased knowledge across a citizenry has a considerable democratizing effect on the activities of government. They suggest that governments operate "more democratically as the range and depth of information held by citizens increases and as the distribution of knowledge becomes more equitable."[6] On *Jeopardy!*, where doctors, lawyers, engineers, and educators compete against students, service workers, public servants, and stay-at-home parents, the importance of expertise quickly gives way to the richer and more meaningful role of the citizen within the context of a much larger and ongoing cultural conversation.

---

[5] According to the US Census Bureau in 2008, with each increasing level of education ranging from "less than a ninth grade education" to the attainment of an "advanced degree," levels of turnout also increased. This relationship is also explored in Steven J. Rosenstone and John Mark Hansen, *Mobilization, Participation, and Democracy in America*, Longman, 2003, as well as in the work of Robert Putnam, who analyzes this correlation from a longitudinal and cross-cultural perspective in his classic work *Bowling Alone*, Yale University Press, 2000.

[6] Michael Delli Carpini and Scott Keeter, *What Americans Know about Politics and Why It Matters*, Yale University Press, 1996, p. 17.

Let's Meet Our Contestants

One more reason *Jeopardy!* helps expand our philosophical understanding of democracy and the citizen is that its competitive framework crowns champions whose skills are intellectual, while also creating a "participatory" environment in which viewers both learn and become involved with the competition. In this respect, *Jeopardy!* not only helps to instill the virtues of knowledge but also the challenge and camaraderie of sport.

There are many books dedicated to the virtues and ethics that are embodied in popular sports, with entire volumes dedicated to the philosophy of basketball, football, baseball, golf, and cycling. Sports challenge competitors to rise above their opponents (and sometimes themselves) in order to win glory. Audiences who consume these sports are presented with gallant images from iconic athletes who train hard, practice harder, and perform at the very limits of human capabilities. These competitions give us heroes that we seek to emulate and practices we applaud as virtuous and worthwhile.

Jeopardy!, and game shows like it, help do for knowledge and intellect what cycling does for strength and stamina, or football does for power and speed. It elevates contestants to a level of public competition and spectacle that draws the attention of sizeable audiences (according to the most recent Nielsen data, *Jeopardy!* remains in the top five syndicated shows in terms of viewership in the United States).[7] It helps to showcase citizens from all walks of life, demonstrating their knowledge across topic areas, and makes information and quick thinking important and accessible.

Jeopardy! and shows like it carve out a segment within the public sphere of popular culture and insert the glorification of knowledge for its own sake, honoring its champions and rewarding contestants with money and prizes. In turn, this helps prime audiences to accept the continued importance of such skills. Moreover, episodes dedicated to collegiate competition help engage the youth, who frequently score among the least knowledgeable and least informed populations in the

---

[7] Robert Seidman, "Syndicated TV Show Ratings," <http://tvbythenumbers.zap2it.com/2012/02/07/syndicated-tv-ratings-judge-judy-wheel-of-fortune-tie-dr-phil-remains-top-talk-show/119103/>.

United States, and make intelligence admirable. *Jeopardy!* helps make smart sexy.

Finally, *Jeopardy!* is emblematic of the popularity of people coming together to engage in competitions of knowledge and trivia, demonstrating how such organized clashes of wits actually inspires camaraderie with others. Such gatherings have positive social and democratic effects. In his 2000 examination of the decline of civic engagement and social capital, *Bowling Alone*, Robert Putnam argued that America is no longer a country of "joiners." Among a variety of other social activities, Putnam expressed sincere concern that people no longer get together to compete with one another or take part in structured activities like bowling leagues.

Putnam concludes that by no longer participating in these social events, individuals are losing their ability to develop social capital (the creation of norms and networks of trust), which in turn has a bad effect on civic engagement as seen in the low levels of voter turnout. Yet, in bars and restaurants across the United States, people gather—sometimes for structured weekly events—and play "Buzztime Trivia Games." These competitions often come with no other reward than "bragging rights" or pride (though sometimes a bartender will also pick up your tab). But what occurs in a larger sense during these competitions is the creation of community and fellowship.

It would be incorrect to assert that the mere existence of *Jeopardy!* will automatically result in more people getting involved within their communities and in democratic politics; the fact that the show has been on, with some interruptions and stoppages for brief periods, since 1964 is enough to speak against such a claim. However, just as we would be wrong to assert that because someone watches the Super Bowl or the March Madness basketball tournament they will automatically start to work out or go join an intramural league, the popularity and consumption of these sports doesn't contribute to the elevation of the skills and virtues that allow contestants to be successful.

The airing of shows like *Jeopardy!* may not automatically translate into an engaged democratic populace, but *Jeopardy!* glorifies those aspects and virtues that have been shown to be so vital to the development of a vibrant democracy. So, whether we play at home or (even better) take our *Jeopardy!* skills out to challenge our friends (and strangers who may become friends) to a round of trivia, the competitive nature of *Jeopardy!* infuses a sense of importance of community and participation.

All Aboard the Brain Bus

Joseph Schumpeter, an economic and democratic theorist, argued that there are many issues within the political arena that are simply too large and complex to have salient meaning within the lives of the democratic citizen. The lack of information possessed by the average person led Schumpeter to conclude that democracy existed merely as a competition of elites with periodic involvement of citizens in elections helping to legitimize, but ultimately not to control, the system.[8]

In a response to criticisms like these, Delli Carpini agrees that the modern world is "bewilderingly complex," but rejects the idea that each citizen must have full and complete mastery of all information relevant to political decision-making to engage in a meaningful way. Summarizing his response, Carpini proclaims:

> I am *not* arguing that contemporary democracy requires that all citizens be expert on all facets of national politics, but I do suggest that the more citizens are passingly informed about the issues of the day, the behavior of political leaders, and the rules under which they operate, the better off they are, the better off *we* are. (http://frank.mtsu.edu/~seig/paper_m_carpini.html)

Jeopardy! is a vehicle of popular entertainment. Like other popular game shows, it is designed to dramatize a form of competition that draws in audiences, and it has done so quite successfully for several decades. Its purpose is not "political" in a traditional sense. However, in the buzzer pressing, category selection, and Daily Double wagers, we get to experience a vital relationship between the citizen and democratic knowledge. Not only do audiences get a chance to learn a little "trivial" information while watching and guessing along with contestants on the show, *Jeopardy!* highlights the value of knowledge and the importance of a diverse exposure and familiarity with the world. And in that, we all are better off.

---

[8] Joseph A. Schumpeter, *Capitalism, Socialism, and Democracy*, second edition, 1947.

13

Survivor Has More to Do with Intelligence than *Jeopardy!*

ELLEN SORG

In the fall of 2004, it wasn't the football season that had people talking, nor was it the new primetime line-up (including hits like *Lost* and *Desperate Housewives*). No, it was one ordinary man, an unexpected television star: Ken Jennings.

In 2004, Ken Jennings began his seventy-four game winning streak on *Jeopardy!*, and his winnings had people talking. As his streak continued, more and more people had thoughts about his reign as the *Jeopardy!* king. In one particular college class I was taking at the time, debates about Jennings and his wins broke out nearly every class. The members of the class were wholeheartedly divided, either as supporters of Jennings or as staunch enemies of the trivia superstar. One classmate even took to wearing t-shirts to class with sayings like "Down with Jennings" and "Jennings: Freak *and* Geek." In response, others broke out the "Ken's a Ten" shirts to counter.

Regardless of which side you fell on, Jennings's run on *Jeopardy!* was exciting, unpredictable, and pure entertainment. The world watched each night to see when or if this streak would end. When it did, it was surreal, unbelievable. After it all ended, however, the spark Jennings's reign ignited was hard to put out. People, perhaps more than ever before, were fascinated with the vast array of knowledge that Jennings had displayed. Many people concluded that Jennings must be one of the most intelligent men alive.

We all believe that game shows like *Jeopardy!* cast only the smartest people around, right? Jennings has made loads of money on the show, as did his successor, Brad Rutter. They have each made hundreds of thousands of dollars and proved their superior knowledge of nearly all possible "categories"— including "Potent Potables" and "Potpourri." But consider this: would Ken Jennings make it on *Survivor*? Maybe not.

While Jennings and other *Jeopardy!* winners may have an abundance of knowledge, are they intelligent enough to survive in the wild? A wide knowledge base allows us to access information on a number of facts; however, it may be that those facts don't translate into the "real world." Contestants on *Jeopardy!* are pushed to show their vast knowledge; as a result, viewers of the show mistakenly perceive the contestants to be models of intelligence. The fact remains that *Jeopardy!* requires few, if any, critical thinking skills. Jennings might be the king of trivia, but he isn't necessarily intelligent; Jennings would perish on *Survivor.*

Knowledge, as We Know It

Most people consider knowledge to be a collection of facts or a familiarity with a particular set of facts. Many dictionaries and online sites might define it in just that way. At the same time, however, there are scores of people who associate knowledge with intelligence. But does having knowledge about facts automatically mean that a person is intelligent?

There are plenty of people who are "smart" about one particular subject, like building houses, but don't know how to do something many people consider simple, like balancing a checkbook. These people are knowledgeable in their given field. But intelligent? No. So why do we confuse knowledge and intelligence so frequently? It may be because we don't have a clear understanding of intelligence. Even shows like *Jeopardy!* support this confusion: this is a show for smart people. Smart people are intelligent. Except that they're not, or at least we can't assume that they are.

Understanding knowledge is something that humans have been wrestling with for centuries, long before *Jeopardy!* took to the air. As early as 540 B.C., scholars were studying how humans acquired and kept hold of knowledge, and theorizing about what humans might do once they gained some knowledge. The likes of philosophers such as Socrates, Plato, and

Aristotle paved the way for the study of knowledge, each coming up with his own theory on knowledge.

Thankfully, taking a look Immanuel Kant's theory of knowledge can help us get further in our understanding of knowledge, and more importantly, how it relates to the contestants on *Jeopardy!* What Kant says, in his *Critique of Pure Reason* (1781), is that knowledge can be broken down into what Horrigan calls "a threefold knowing power: sensibility, intellect and reason."[1] Kant describes these knowing powers as the Transcendental Aesthetic, the Transcendental Analytic, and the Transcendental Dialectic. For our use in understanding knowledge as it relates to *Jeopardy!,* all we really need to talk about right now is the Transcendental Aesthetic, or sensibility.

Kant thought that we wouldn't be able to make any sense of the world unless we were equipped with certain ways of thinking, for example the notions of space and time. It's not possible to perceive the world unless we're already equipped with these fundamental notions. In other words, we need both space and time to make any sort of understanding of facts. But, as humans, we can only know things as they appear to the human mind. So knowledge of facts requires reason, as well as merely taking in impressions through our senses.

But I'm Intelligent, Right?

Since we know (at least according to Kant) that knowledge is a combination of sensory experience and of reason, it makes sense that an individual would have to go even further in their thinking to be considered intelligent. What happens next is that "the intellect takes in these finished products of sensation" and proceeds to mold and shape them into a new form—a form on which the intellect can act. This is what Kant calls the Transcendental Analytic.

It's hard to say whether the contestants on *Jeopardy!* reach this point in their thinking. Certainly, they invoke the knowledge they have gained through reason and experience, but do they then act as a result of that knowledge? Maybe, but I think the most action we see from the contestants is with the signal-

---

[1] Paul Gerard Horrigan, *Epistemology: An Introduction to the Philosophy of Knowledge*, Amazon, 2007, pp. 65–66.

ing buttons. Some people might claim that pushing the signaling button is the kind of action Kant was describing, but I think that could be a bit of a stretch. We can't say that those who appear on *Jeopardy!* truly *act* on their knowledge.

Kant argues that reason is useful only in that it has a regulative property. Reason can be of great importance—at least, when you're participating in the world. On *Jeopardy!*, reason isn't necessarily a factor for you to become a winner. A contestant has to consider the answer and if the question fits, but it certainly seems a stretch to say that the contestants are truly "reasoning" when providing answers to the *Jeopardy!* clues.

Let's Be Practical

Some consider intelligence not as a basic conclusion of knowledge, but as an entity of its own. A group of thinkers identified as pragmatists consider thought to gain its "value and meaning in its practical consequences." So thought alone doesn't mean much until there is some sort of action to validate the thought.

Charles S. Peirce, who has been called "'the most original, versatile, and comprehensive' intellect that America has yet produced"[2] led the pragmatist movement. In Peirce's work, as well as in the work of another famous pragmatist William James, the goal is to "go beyond the dualistic approach to the relationship between mind and world"[3] Peirce and James wanted to show that the ideas of reason and will are not in direct competition with one another; instead, there is room for reasoning and for free will—a person can believe in the facts of science while also believing in morals and ideals.

The contestants on *Jeopardy!* don't have to worry too much about these concepts, as the trivia show doesn't ask its contestants to do anything more than provide answers to clues—doing so does not require the contestant to consider himself or herself outside of Sony Picture Studios. There is no moral dilemma, no worry about ideals versus facts, and as a result, no real need for *intelligence*. Pragmatism holds that a thought is true, not because it agrees with some extra-mental reality, but

---

[2] Gary Richmond, *Journal of Cultural and Media Studies* (2008), p. 156.
[3] Rosa M. Calcaterra, *Journal of Speculative Philosophy* (2011), p. 413.

because it works out right when it is applied. In the case of the game show, contestants only need to figure out that a fact agrees with a particular given clue.

I Will Survive

A player on *Jeopardy!* can be called knowledgeable, but it's a stretch to call these contestants intelligent, as there has been no real application of their knowledge. A show like *Jeopardy!* simply does not ask its contestants to prove their intelligence. On the other hand, another popular CBS show, *Survivor,* asks its contestants to do just that.

Survivor isn't known as a game that involves especially intelligent people; in fact, most of the cast members see their biggest threats in terms of physical, rather than mental, prowess. And yet, what *Survivor*, unlike *Jeopardy!*, truly requires is intelligence. The producers of *Survivor* would be hard-pressed to find a person as knowledgeable as Ken Jennings (okay, maybe Brad Rutter), but it's really unlikely that Jennings would win the game, and that's not because of his physical strength. Instead, it's because Jennings isn't asked in the multiple games of trivia he plays to act on his knowledge or concretely apply the knowledge in any way. All Jennings has to do to succeed in a quiz show is to recall facts. Much more is required of a *Survivor* champion.

Ken Jennings can tell you a lot of facts about fire—when the first fire was built, the proper ratio of heat, oxygen, and fuel that must exist to create it, who forwarded the invention of fire. However, can Ken Jennings start a fire in the wilderness without a match or other pre-existing source of flame? I don't know, but my money is on 'No'. Jennings is a busy man who probably hasn't had the time to apply his knowledge of fire to the actual building of a fire. Even if Jennings can relate every step necessary in creating fire, he still may not be able to create fire himself. As a result, something as basic as fire-building could be a downfall in Jennings's *Survivor* game. It's not necessarily true that the winner of the game has to be able to start a fire, but it sure gives someone an advantage. Contestants without this skill are generally cold and hungry, and they have to rely upon the skills of other players, which can be dangerous, at least in terms of game-playing.

On *Jeopardy!*, contestants are not asked to do much more than provide answers to clues; *Survivor,* on the other hand, asks contestant to "Outwit, Outplay, and Outlast." To do this, contestants must be able to build structures in which to live, find and cook much of their own food, match wits with other contestants, compete in physical competitions, and outplay the other cast members with a great social game. These tasks are those which require intelligence. On *Survivor* a player must be willing to modify their conduct in order to move forward in the game. The player must also be able to reflect on the mistakes made throughout the game, and figure out how to change those mistakes into goals that are workable for the whole group. These are acts of intelligence.

In each case, the player must go beyond the invocation of knowledge to actual application and reflection. According to Gary Richmond, "Peirce considered the ultimate goal of pragmatism to be the modification of conduct, the central idea being that . . . communities could more and more find agreeable goals, principles, and practices" (p. 159). Pragmatism sees knowledge as being valuable insofar as it can be acted upon.

Jennings would be at an immediate loss on *Survivor* in that he has only demonstrated the ability to recall facts, not the ability to apply a particular idea to situation. Can Jennings put together a dwelling that will hold through thirty-nine days of jungle living? Can Jennings catch a bird or a fish, prepare it, and cook it? There seems no necessary reason to believe that the answer to either of those questions would be 'Yes'. The recollection of facts is not nearly enough to survive on *Survivor.*

Knowledge is what it takes to win *Jeopardy!*, while intelligence is what it takes to win *Survivor*. I have nothing against Jennings; he seems to be a very nice and extremely knowledgeable person, but he hasn't demonstrated that he is capable of taking his knowledge beyond the first stage of Kant's theory, the Transcendental Aesthetic, to intellect or the ability to act.

Kim Spradlin Beats Ken Jennings

In the game of *Jeopardy!*, knowledge reigns supreme, and all else can fall by the wayside. As we saw in 2004, a vast array of knowledge, and the ability to invoke that knowledge in a swift manner is what it takes to win the game. Ken Jennings took the game by storm, and he racked up a significant amount of money in the process. But while Jennings proved he has a level of knowledge that is nearly unprecedented, he did nothing to prove his intelligence.

Outside of Sony Picture Studios, there's no guarantee that Jennings can move beyond his knowledge base to the practical application of knowledge. He isn't testing theories, considering ideas in relation to situations, or changing his own conduct as a result of self-reflection. All he is doing is providing answers to the clues given. The clues are often difficult and obscure, but they do not require a contestant to think further than merely to the correct answer.

In contrast, though *Survivor* isn't really known as a game that involves only smart people—and sometimes the smartest people don't win—what the game really asks of its contestants is that they use intelligence to beat out the other competitors. The winner really doesn't have to be the most physically strong member of the group; if a cast member can figure out ways to provide food, shelter, and win at competitions, that cast member can win.

As recently as the 2012 season of the show, *Survivor: One World,* the winner of the game was certainly not the most physically gifted of the group. Kim Spradlin, a young woman from Texas, took the crown as Sole Survivor. It was not her physical strength, but her mental strength, that earned her the title. For sure, Spradlin was able to catch food when she needed to, but she was also able to apply her knowledge of the game to nearly every situation in which she found herself. She didn't make fatal *Survivor* errors (backstabbing, talking in circles, creating panic); instead, Spradlin was cool and calculated in the way she dealt with other players. She spoke in a way that was open without revealing all of her true intentions, and she put rumors to rest in order to preserve her own safety. These are the acts of an intelligent person. The way she was able to craft her game through careful thinking and consideration led to her ultimate *Survivor* victory. Nearly all of the jury members cast their votes for Spradlin; they recognized her game-playing ability, maybe not while they were with her in the game, but certainly afterward.

For Jennings, facts are all that matter, but for Spradlin, facts don't really matter at all. The results, for both, are similar: both played games at which they won. But the way they got to those ends is vastly different. Jennings was only required to access knowledge; certainly, he had a lot of fact-based knowledge to access, but all he had to do was recall a fact as the result of a given clue. Kim Spradlin, on the other hand, had to push to her mental limits to apply her knowledge to the game of *Survivor*. This application of knowledge can be seen as what a pragmatist would view as intelligence. Spradlin worked within the context of a real situation, and doing so required intelligence.

It may be true that Spradlin doesn't have the stock of knowledge necessary to win on *Jeopardy!,* but in the same way, Ken Jennings seems in no way necessarily prepared to win the game of *Survivor*. While both games require capable contestants, only one requires its contestants to be intelligent. Only knowledge is necessary when pursuing a win on *Jeopardy!* Intelligence is what it takes to win *Survivor*. Knowledge is a separate concept from intelligence, and we can see the difference by keeping an eye on two of the most popular game shows on television, *Survivor* and *Jeopardy!*

14
This Question Is False

GEORGE A. REISCH

FRANCIS HERBERT BRADLEY: [*to himself*] Well *this* is far from ideal. I arrived on time and I've now been sitting in this room for almost an hour. It figures that Wittgenstein would be late, but Russell? And these bloody doughnuts, or whatever they call them. I don't think I've ever tasted anything so bloody awful.

He thumbs through a People *magazine as if it were written in some unknown language.*

A door opens and Bertrand Russell steps halfway in.

BERTRAND RUSSELL: Hello, I'm looking for the "the green room." Is this it?

BRADLEY: *Bertie*!

RUSSELL: *Bradley*! My, hasn't it been *a long time*? I don't think I've heard from you since 1911 or so, when I explained why you were wrong to insist that wholes cannot be fully analyzed into their constituents.

BRADLEY: Well, that's not how I remember it. And I remain convinced as ever that your penchant for "analysis" or, what do they call it nowadays, 'analytical philosophy' is simply sterile for understanding reality and experience.

RUSSELL: Oh Bradley, let this dead horse rest, will you? Philosophy has long ago *moved on* past the idealism you always defended. And it's *still moving*. Have you followed the ups and downs of logical empiricism? Say, what about Wittgenstein's latest unpublished grumblings? Why I hear he's now saying that one can't even. . .

Bradley looks past Russell to the door behind him, slowly, nervously opening.

BRADLEY: Speak of the devil. Wittgenstein!

RUSSELL: [*walking over to greet Wittgenstein*] Ludwig! How very nice to see you!

Wittgenstein glances nervously about the room as he returns their greetings.

LUDWIG WITTGENSTEIN: Hello, Bertie, hello Bradley.

BRADLEY: So you found the green room. Rather silly, don't you think? There's nothing green in it.

Russell chuckles along with Bradley. But Wittgenstein furrows his brow and stares directly at Bradley.

WITTGENSTEIN: Should there be something green?

RUSSELL: Well it's surely remarkable, don't you think? All this talk of the "the green room" by the producers and the make-up people, and yet here we are amidst white walls and brown leather furniture.

WITTGENSTEIN: Oh Bertie, are you *still* mired in your theory of descriptions? As if words and language had some precise, specifiable relationship to the world? It's not physics, you know. . . .

BRADLEY: Oh, Ludwig, relax. We're just making conversation, really, before our television debut. I don't know about you two, but I've been a little nervous. I realize it's just a game that is broadcast on television, but I was hoping this appearance on *Jeopardy!* might help revive some interest in ideali . . .

WITTGENSTEIN: [*interrupting*]: "Just a game!" Bradley. You say, "*just* a game." But games are all there is. This "green room" is a perfect example. It's named "the green room" precisely because that's what the people in this business call it, just like plumbers have funny names for their tools and philosophers have names for different beliefs and methods. It doesn't have to be *green* any more than a realist philosopher is *real*.

BRADLEY: Well that's "real" in a different sense, of course.

WITTGENSTEIN: Of course. But isn't that the point: the different senses that words have belong to the different rules and customs of the language game being played. So you see, you can't say *Jeopardy!* is "just a game" then, can you?

RUSSELL: Ludwig, be serious. Bradley isn't as confused as you say he is—on *this* matter, at least. In fact the meaning of theatrical "green rooms" did once involve the color green—of the grass on which performers enacted a play, for instance.

WITTGENSTEIN: As usual, Russell, you entirely misunderstand me. I am not saying that the meaning cannot or did not have something to do with the color green; I'm saying that it *need* not, unless you remain wedded to some *correspondence* theory of meaning, as if "green room" somehow *corresponds* to the thing it names.

BRADLEY: Okay Ludwig. Let me see if I understand you. Because appearances and reality interpenetrate within the whole of the Absolute, names can bear many relations to. . . .

WITTGENSTEIN: No! Bradley. Bloody Christ! Let's not play *that* game. It's because language is more complicated than philosophers ever suspected; even my *Tractatus* and Russell's theory of logical atomism rest on the illusion that language . . .

The door opens again and Alex Trebek walks in.

ALEX TREBEK: Gentlemen! I have been looking forward to today's taping for *months*! I am so glad to see you all here. I'm the show's host, Alex Trebek, and you must be Francis Herbert Bradley [*he shakes Bradley's outstretched hand*].

RUSSELL: Hello, I'm Bertie Russell. [*They shake hands.*]

TREBEK: Russell, pleased to meet you! And, of course, Ludwig Wittgenstein. I never *dreamed* all those years ago when I was studying your *Tractatus* in college that I would ever find myself working with you.

Wittgenstein's eyebrows go up at the phrase "working with you."

TREBEK: So, how is your career going?

Wittgenstein's eyebrows rise again, having never thought of his "work" as a "career". He replies slowly, and with less confidence, having been thrown off by Trebek's sunny, Hollywood collegiality.

WITTGENSTEIN: Well, um, as I was saying to Bradley and Russell here. I've come to the conclusion of late that much of philosophy, even my *Tractatus*, rests on some, um, confusions about the nature of the relationship between language and the world.

TREBEK: We've got a few minutes before our taping starts. I'd *love* to hear your thoughts, Ludwig.

WITTGENSTEIN: Right, well, it's partly a problem of meaning, really. You see we ordinarily presuppose that the things we talk about can be precisely defined, but in fact they usually can't. The meaning of a word is not what it refers to, but rather the way it is *used* . . . and here it's usually no longer a case of reference or simple definition. *What* is a rule? For example, or what is a *game*? [*glancing at Bradley*] Bradley here was just carrying on as if our event here today was "just a game" that was somehow categorically different from other things that are not games. But I've discovered instead that our definitions rest instead on "family resemblances" that are blurry and not sharp at all. You can't specify a sharp definition of "game," because the things we call "games" do not share any one set of properties. They are more like the members of a family, some of whom share the shape of a nose, others of whom have a similar gait, and others of whom may share similar eyebrows, and so on. But no member of a family shares all these properties, so those properties cannot provide us with a sharp definition of "game."

RUSSELL: Well there's no game about which of *these* . . . what are they called [*looking at the side of the brightly colored box*] *donuts* I'm going to eat. [*He picks up a Boston Cream, eyes it suspiciously, and takes a bite.*]

WITTGENSTEIN: But you'd be wrong there, Russell. Lots of games require players to make choices, as you just did. I'm sure our friends at Dunkin' Donuts have people like you in mind when they choose what donuts they are going to create . . .

TREBEK: And *Jeopardy!* is all about choices—categories, how much to wager . . .

WITTGENSTEIN: Right, so . . . depending on what game-like properties you have in mind, it's not so clear that picking a donut is *not* a game, or *part* of a game of some kind.

RUSSELL: Ludwig, Ludwig! [*Russell is chewing and swallowing.*] Yes, of course—no one is so silly as to believe that games are really as simple as a science experiment with only a few ingredients and controlled variables. But you yourself, a former engineer, know very well the value of approaching matters scientifically and trying to keep things simple and clear. . .

WITTGENSTEIN: [*interrupting Russell*] Yes, I do know science, and I can see how it misleads philosophers like you to reduce explanations and definitions to *the smallest number* of things. But in fact you will see if you pay sufficient attention that the relevant properties of things on which our use of language depends can be *countless*. You suppose things *must* be a certain way in order to satisfy your craving for simplicity and generality, but I say *look and see* if they are really that way. This craving is *the real source* of metaphysics, it leads the philosopher into *complete* darkness, and I simply refuse to indulge this wretched habit!

TREBEK: [*trying to calm Wittgenstein down and smooth things over*] Well, hopefully you three can put your differences aside for today. Now, have they gone over the rules with you? You all know that nobody on the set, even myself, knows the categories or clues in advance. Have they told you how to use the signaling device? [*They all nod.*] Now, the game has three rounds, *Jeopardy!*, *Double Jeopardy!*, and *Final* . . .

RUSSELL: [*interrupting and ignoring Trebek*] Ludwig, I really think you're creating your own confused *metaphysics*. It's one thing to play a game and another entirely different thing to *define* games; it's one thing to adhere to a rule, another to define what a rule *is*. You seem altogether unable to *separate these things* with the result that you're ever so tortured personally and put off by those persons who *can*! I mean, really, of all people I myself am quite aware of how difficult these matters of definition and meaning can be— but not for a moment am I going to conclude that all this complexity means analytic philosophy is finished, washed up, and just a matter of solving linguistic puzzles or, how do you put it now, 'showing the fly out of the fly bottle.'

WITTGENSTEIN: Oh *honestly*, Russell, you're living in your past. Now you're going to tell me it comes down to your *theory of types*, I suppose, that 'the set of all sets that do not contain themselves as members' or even 'this sentence is false' are not paradoxical once we stipulate that there are separate *kinds of things* or types of sets or types of sentences that coexist without mingling and overlapping. But this is precisely the kind of distinction that we can't make. . . .

There is a loud knock on the door. "Two Minutes!" a production assistant outside announces. Trebek begins herding the philosophers out of the green room as the argument continues.

RUSSELL: Yes, exactly, well . . . in a way, yes. There are different types of activities and concerns that we set for ourselves with the result that we need not, at every minute of the day, attend to every one of them. Sometimes you simply have to *play* a game, as we are about to, and not worry about *defining* it, or what kind of definition is possible, or what kind of puzzles lie in store.

JOHNNY GILBERT: This is *Jeopardy!* Lets meet today's contestants. A teacher and former aeronautical engineer from Austria, Ludwig Wittgenstein. A British professor of philosophy and recipient of the Order of Merit, Francis Herbert Bradley. And our returning champion, a philosopher, logician, and social critic from Cambridge University, Bertrand Russell. [*applause*]

And now our host, Alex Trebek!

TREBEK: Thank you Johnny Gilbert. Ladies and Gentlemen, welcome to *Jeopardy!* I am sure you all notice that the biggest smile among our contestants today belongs to our returning champion Lord Russell. [*turns to Russell*] Why is that, Lord Russell?

RUSSELL: Well, I'm just so pleased to be competing not only against my former student, Mr. Wittgenstein, but also Professor Bradley who was once *my* teacher.

TREBEK: Okay, well it is an honor for us to host all three of you eminent philosophers on today's show. Let's get to today's categories which are:

Reality [*Ding*]
Knowledge [*Ding*]
Logic [*Ding*]
Ethics [*Ding*]
Psychology, No Thank You [*Ding*]
and Space and Time [*Ding*]

Lord Russell, as returning champion, you can lead us off.

RUSSELL: I'll take Knowledge for $400, Alex.

TREBEK: If you truly had some, *this* ancient figure is believed to have said, you couldn't understand it.

[*Buzz. Wittgenstein's podium lights up*]

TREBEK: [*continuing*] Wittgenstein!

WITTGENSTEIN: Bradley?

Bradley appears to be puzzled as to what Wittgenstein could mean by saying that. Wittgenstein's score drops to –400 as Russell buzzes in.

TREBEK: Russell.

RUSSELL: Who is Gorgias?

TREBEK: Right, Plato's Gorgias. That gives you a score of 400.

RUSSELL: I'll take Space and Time for $500, please.

TREBEK: If the theory of general relativity is correct, *this massive object* should detectably bend starlight.

Bradley buzzes in.

TREBEK: Bradley!

BRADLEY: What is The Absolute?

TREBEK: No.

Bradley's score drops to -500 and he looks indignant that his answer is not correct. Wittgenstein buzzes in.

TREBEK: Wittgenstein.

WITTGENSTEIN: Bradley?

TREBEK: No, that brings Wittgenstein's score to minus 900. [*Buzz*] Russell!

RUSSELL: What is the sun?

TREBEK: That is correct, Russell, for a total of 900.

Fearing that Wittgenstein is toying with the game and deliberately flouting the rules, Trebek keeps his cool and offers a gentle warning.

TREBEK: [continuing] And let me remind Wittgenstein that answers on *Jeopardy!* must be given in the form of a question. Russell the board remains in your control.

RUSSELL: I'll take Reality for $300.

TREBEK: The metaphysical theory positing the existence of one and only one substance.

Russell, Wittgenstein, and Bradley all attempt to buzz in. Bradley's registers first.

TREBEK: Bradley!

BRADLEY: What is monism? [*Bradley is so confident his voice does not rise at the end of his answer.*]

TREBEK: That's correct, as you yourself would no doubt agree! [*Bradley's score increases to –200.*]

[*Beep Beep Beeeeep*]

TREBEK: Ah, there's the buzzer. And *that* ladies and gentlemen concludes this first round of Jeopardy, with Bradley at minus 200 dollars, Wittgenstein at minus 900, and Russell at 900. Let's take a little time to meet our contestants shall we? Russell, you earlier told us about your relationship with Bradley. Why, of course, you began your career as an idealist, didn't you. But then you helped lead the so-called "revolt against idealism," in the 1910s and 1920s, is that correct?

Bradley, scowling, looks eager to say something.

RUSSELL: Yes, so it is often said. I prefer to think of it as that I helped found modern philosophy, *proper*.

TREBEK: Professor Bradley. You were a prominent *metaphysician*, as I understand it. Tell us, what does that mean?

BRADLEY: Well, it's really quite simple. I merely set out to offer some corrections to Hegel's response to Kant, specifically regarding the extent to which Reality comes *into* knowledge and is one Absolute Experience, self-pervading, and, so you see, superior to mere relations.

Russell stares blankly. Wittgenstein can't even listen. He just stares down intently at his podium, as if he's trying to be polite at Idealism's funeral.

TREBEK: [*trying not to be overly polite*] I see, yes. Now, Mr. Wittgenstein, is it true that your famous book, *Tractatus Logico-Philosophicus* was written while you were a prisoner of war in Italy?

WITTGENSTEIN: Yes, some of it was. I was then corresponding with Russell here [*gestures to Russell*] who later arranged for its publication in England.

TREBEK: Fascinating. And you are currently at work on a new project, I understand.

WITTGENSTEIN: Yes, I have revised many of my former views, largely because I have lately found that I cannot unify them into any kind of system or logical program. Philosophy can never really be, I think, more than isolated remarks to clarify and hopefully resolve language's many puzzles.

TREBEK: Russell is shaking his head. I only wish our studio audience could have heard your earlier, shall we say, *heated* conversation in the green room. Well, yes! Let's move to our Double Jeopardy! round with *these* new categories!

You Don't Say [*Ding*]
Categorize This! [*Ding*]
Kant Can't [*Ding*]
Dewey or Don't We? [*Ding*]
Time's Up [*Ding*]

Bradley, you answered the last question correctly so you can begin.

BRADLEY: Yes, um, I'll take You Don't Say for $800.

TREBEK: Were it to suddenly speak to us, we could not understand it.

All three pump their hand-held buzzers. Russell's podium lights up.

TREBEK: Russell

RUSSELL: [*hesitantly*] What is Kant's *noumenon*? [*Russell's score falls to 100.*]

TREBEK: No. [*Bradley's podium lights up.*] Bradley.

BRADLEY: What is The Absolute? [*Bradley's score falls to -1,000.*]

TREBEK: No. [*Wittgenstein buzzes.*] Wittgenstein.

WITTGENSTEIN: What is a lion?

TREBEK: That is correct for $800, bringing you to −100 and you control the board.

Wittgenstein seems to have found his stride. Russell and Bradley look at each other quizzically as if they both wonder, 'a lion?'

WITTGENSTEIN: I'll take You Don't Say for $1,000.

Ding Ding Ding

TREBEK: Ah, the Daily Double! Now, Wittgenstein, you may wager up to one thousand dollars.

WITTGENSTEIN: I will wager one thousand.

TREBEK: Alright then, the clue is: About this kind of experience, nothing at all can be said.

WITTGENSTEIN: What is the mystical.

TREBEK: That is correct! And this brings you to 900, tied with Russell, while . . .

[*Ding*]

Oh, there goes our time for this round. Now we enter Final Jeopardy! where, I am afraid, Professor Bradley, you are disqualified because with your score of minus one thousand you have no money to wager. [*Bradley leaves the stage.*]

So, that leaves us with Wittgenstein and Russell, each with nine hundred dollars, heading into Final Jeopardy! where our category is: *Definitions*, and our remaining contestants must decide how much they will wager.

As they pick up their pens to place their wagers, Russell seems unfazed but Wittgenstein is apprehensive. Definitions? *he wonders. That could go in many different directions. He slowly writes down his wager and puts his pen down.*

TREBEK: Let's look at the clue, shall we? It is: "An activity engaged in for diversion or amusement."

Trebek visibly marvels at this coincidence. As the Final Jeopardy! *theme music begins to ring throughout the studio, Russell confidently jots down his answer, places down his pen, and folds his hands. Wittgenstein, however, is struggling. He begins to write, then stops. He crosses something out and starts writing again. He puts his pen down, glances warily at Russell next to him and then, with a flash of inspiration, picks up his pen, crosses out what he had written, and furiously writes another answer. He finishes in the nick of time.*

TREBEK: Let's go to our champion, Bertrand Russell. Russell did you give the answer?

The screen on Russell's podium illuminates to read, What is a game?

TREBEK: That is correct. And you wagered . . . $900 to bring you to a total of $1,800. Wittgenstein, you wrote . . .

Wittgenstein's screen illuminates to read:

> What is a ~~ga~~
> What is ~~a thing with a family resemblance to other gam~~
> What is a MISLEADING ANSWER to the question 'What is a game?'"?

TREBEK: No, I'm sorry. . .

Back in the green room, Wittgenstein and Russell are gathering their coats and things preparing to leave the studio.

WITTGENSTEIN: [*with detectable sarcasm, to himself*] Right, well. "Sometimes you just have to *play* a game, and not worry about *defining* it."

RUSSELL: Um, ah. What is a circumstance that is *usually* true?

WITTGENSTEIN: Well, this was not a usual circumstance, was it?

RUSSELL: No, but I'm afraid I have to agree with the judges.

WITTGENSTEIN: Quelle Surprise!

RUSSELL: Of course answers on *Jeopardy!* can't be self-referential; they must answer the clue and *only* the clue. One can't *play* the game and offer critical remarks about the suppositions on which the clues depend *at the same time.*

WITTGENSTEIN: But of course one can; that's what I just *did*.

RUSSELL: Yes, and as a result you lost the game.

WITTGENSTEIN: Not at all. I merely spent a few hours of diversion and amusement with some old friends. In fact . . . In *fact*, Bertie, it was very nice to work again with you and Bradley and that Trebek fellow. Until next time . . .

Wittgenstein leaves the green room. Russell looks to see if there are any donuts left.[1]

---

[1] On the early Bradley-Russell dispute over the analysis of wholes, see Ray Monk, *Ludwig Wittgenstein: The Duty of Genius*, 1990, p. 198. On Wittgenstein's conception of "language games," see Wittgenstein, *Philosophical Investigations (PI)*, Macmillan, 1953, §23; on rejection of correspondence theories of meaning, *PI* §40; on criticism of his own *Tractatus*, see Wittgenstein, *The Blue and Brown Books (BB)* Harper, p. 31; on family resemblances and the definition of games, see *PI* §65–72; on the necessity to "look and see" versus trusting definitions, see *PI* §66; on a scientific "craving" misleading philosophy into "complete darkness," *BB* p. 18; on philosophy and the "fly bottle," *PI* §309. On Russell's theory of types as a response to paradoxes of self-reference, see "Russell's Paradox" at *Stanford Encyclopedia of Philosophy*. Bradley's conception of 'self-pervading Absolute Experience,' is quoted from Bradley, *Appearance and Reality*, London, 1893, p. 552. On the Russell-Wittgenstein correspondence and the publication of the *Tractatus,* see Monk, *Duty of Genius*, chapter 8. On Wittgenstein's post-Tractarian view of philosophy as unconnected remarks, see *PI*, preface. On a talking lion that we could not understand, see *PI*, p. 223.

I'll Take Potpourri, Alex

Here are the Answers
(For the Questions, see page 187)

(For the Questions, see page 187)

1. This philosopher supposedly hugged a horse which was being whipped by its owner.

2. It's the paradox embodied in the claim, "This sentence is false."

3. A scandalous eighteenth-century story about a beehive by this London doctor influenced subsequent moral philosophy.

4. This philosopher's *Guide for the Perplexed* developed Jewish theology by harmonizing it with Aristotle's ideas.

5. He's the first philosopher in the history of Western philosophy.

6. This thirteenth-century philosopher outlined five ways to prove the existence of God.

7. He said, "Be a philosopher; but, amidst all your philosophy, be still a man."

8. It's also known as the law of parsimony or economy.

9. This eighteenth-century Presbyterian minister came up with a simple mathematical formula which is now the cornerstone of the subjectivist approach to probability.

10. This great philosophical work was said by its author to have fallen "still-born from the press."

11. She lived in Roman-ruled Egypt and was killed by a Coptic Christian mob who blamed her for religious turmoil.

12. Developed in 1957, this design was originally called Neue Haas Grotesk.

13. He's the father of *utilitarianism*, arguing that "it is the greatest happiness of the greatest number that is the measure of right and wrong."

14. He wrote: "I know of no country in which there is so little independence of mind and real freedom of discussion as in America."

15. He is considered by many to have invented the modern idea of civil disobedience.

16. This imaginative story by Plato is one of the oldest discussions of the difference between a life of illusions and a life of wisdom.

17. These unproved speculations, designed to explain aspects of the natural world, were famously rejected by natural philosopher Isaac Newton.

18. This philosopher had a close shave in 1328 when he and his friends absconded from Avignon with the seal of the Franciscan Order.

19. Just not worth living, according to Socrates.

20. A formerly living being whom "we have killed," according to Friedrich Nietzsche.

21. This animal, standing on the back of another, that is standing on the back of yet another "all the way down," is often used to symbolize an infinite regress in metaphysics.

22. This philosopher developed "the social contract" in order to understand the relationship between societies and their governments.

23. Had George Berkeley written *Hamlet*, the play's famous question might have taken this idealistic metaphysical slant.

24. Exactly 299,792,458 meters per second.

25. This philosophical donkey sometimes had trouble making decisions.

26. He is the second philosopher in the history of Western philosophy.

27. He's a well-known philosopher, no doubt, but he also invented analytic geometry.

28. Written in A.D. 397–398, this work talks about plenty of sex, crime, alcohol, and even an illegitimate son begotten by its author.

29. He said that you can't step in the same river twice.

30. This person made the surprising claim that, "Socrates is the wisest man in Athens."

Meet the Clue Crew

FRANKLIN ALLAIRE is a PhD student in Educational Foundations in the College of Education at the University of Hawaiʻi at Mānoa. His interests include science education, identity theory and salience, and post-structural relationships between ontology and epistemology. In his spare time he enjoys running, photography, and stunning friends, students and colleagues alike into silence with annoyingly useless trivia and (occasionally made up) facts. Never a contestant on *Jeopardy!*, Franklin looks forward to the day when he'll be able to wear his costume that won him second prize in an Alex Trebek look-alike contest in a battle of wits with other *Jeopardy! and Philosophy* authors.

ROBERT ARP has interests in Philosophy and Pop Culture and ontology in the information-science sense. He is the author or editor of numerous books, book chapters, and articles in these realms. See his website at: robertarp.webs.com. Why in the F does it have to be *Jeopardy!* with an exclamation point, instead of simple, Jeopardy? Not with the question mark, of course . . . that's just part of my question.

You: "Sorites Biographies for $200." Alex: "This university, founded in 1869 as a normal school is currently in the middle of nowhere." You: "Er, umm, what is Southern Illinois University Carbondale?" Alex: Correct. You: "Sorites Biographies for $400." Alex: "This obscure American academic doesn't subscribe to cable, has no satellite dish, and lives in the middle of nowhere, where he writes semi-philosophical literature obsessively." You: "Er, umm, who is **RANDALL AUXIER**?" Alex: "I'm sorry, that is incorrect. The right question is 'Who is no one you'd care to read about?'"

JOSEPH J. FOY is the Associate Dean of the University of Wisconsin-Waukesha, and member of the political science department of the University of Wisconsin Colleges. He is the editor of *Homer Simpson*

Goes to Washington: American Politics through Popular Culture and *SpongeBob SquarePants and Philosophy: Soaking Up Secrets Under the Sea!* Foy is also the co-editor of *Homer Simpson Marches on Washington: Dissent through American Popular Culture* and a forthcoming collection on political philosophy contained in movies, television, music, and consumer culture. He has contributed chapters in collections on *The Hunger Games*, *True Blood*, *Star Trek*, *The X-Files*, the music of the Rolling Stones, and the creative works of Joss Whedon, Steven Spielberg, J.J. Abrams and Ang Lee. Foy can also say with absolute confidence that Archibald Leach, Bernard Schwartz, and Lucille LeSueur have never been in his kitchen.

In 2004, **KEN JENNINGS** was an anonymous software engineer from Salt Lake City, Utah, when he notched up seventy-four consecutive *Jeopardy!* wins, still an American game show record. Since then, he has written four books: *Brainiac: Adventures in the Curious, Competitive, Compulsive World of Trivia Buffs*; *Ken Jennings's Trivia Almanac: 8,888 Questions in 365 Days*; *Maphead: Charting the Weird, Wide World of Geography Wonks*; and *Because I Said So!: The Truth Behind the Myths, Tales, and Warnings Every Generation Passes Down to Its Kids*. He lives in Seattle with his family.

MATT KOHLSTEDT is completing his PhD in American Studies at The George Washington University. In 2009, he won five games of *Jeopardy!* and was a semifinalist in that year's Tournament of Champions. He would like to assure his current and former teachers that he knows how many articles are in the US Constitution. And, since everyone asks, no, he didn't get to hang out with Alex, but he did seem like a good dude during their limited interactions. (He's also glad to hear Alex is back at work after his heart attack.) Having not done so on the show itself, Matt would like to credit his parents and grandparents for their help and inspiration. He lives in Madison, Wisconsin, with his wife, dog, and, as of August 2012, his first child (and 2029 Teen Tournament sensation).

RICK MAYOCK drives by the *Jeopardy!* studio at Sony Pictures every day on his way to work at West LA College, which reminds him to prepare his philosophy lecture in the form of a question. He's a frequent contributor to volumes on philosophy and popular culture, including *The Beatles and Philosophy: Nothing You Can Think that Can't Be Thunk*, *The Rolling Stones and Philosophy: It's Just a Thought Away*, and *The Catcher in the Rye and Philosophy: A Book for Bastards, Morons, and Madmen*.

Being a long time professor of Classical and Medieval Rhetoric at UC Berkeley has thoroughly prepared **DANIEL MELIA** to answer in the form of a question. Socrates does little else, and encouraging students to construct legitimate Aristotelian syllogisms requires constant answers formed as questions ("What is an undistributed middle term?") With a second professorial hat in Celtic Studies, information about historical linguistics ("Those Darned Etruscans"), Celtic languages, Gaul, Rome, and other ancient and modern cultures has to fit into his head as well. Undergraduate studies in the Victorian period, and pre-med courses have also left their residue of trivia, although a significant portion of everything he knows was acquired in the 1960s at the Phillips Exeter Academy. A strong amateur interest in strong drink (he sponsors a student-led course on the history of scotch whisky) helps with "Potent Potables" and an intermittent career as a volunteer supernumerary ("spear carrier") at the San Francisco Opera would have helped had he ever had a shot at the "Dreaded Opera Category." He and his wife, Dara Hellman, who were married on the *Jeopardy!* set, live in Berkeley with their two toy poodles. His son, who first encouraged him to try out for the show, is a Navy veteran and student who lives in New Orleans.

NICOLAS MICHAUD teaches philosophy in Jacksonville, Florida. He has a particular love for the study of Machine Intelligence and has taught numerous courses on the subject. However, it was not until the computer program, "Watson," kicked humanity's butt on *Jeopardy!* that Nick realized the robot apocalypse is nigh. In order to prepare for this event, he suggests buying lots and lots of cookies . . . because 1. our robot overlords will have no use for them, and 2. cookies make everything better.

GEORGE REISCH is the series editor of the Popular Culture and Philosophy series. He teaches philosophy and intellectual history in Northwestern University's School of Continuing Studies and researches the history of philosophy of science in the cold war.

TIMOTHY SEXTON was named Associated Content's (now Yahoo! Contributor Network) inaugural Writer of the Year just four years after earning his BA in English from the University of West Florida. He currently writes two daily columns for Yahoo! Movies and regularly contributes on a variety of topics and subjects related to entertainment. He is the author of two novels and a chapter in *Sherlock Holmes and Philosophy: The Footprints of a Gigantic Mind*. His ambition is not to one day become a *Jeopardy!* contestant, but to become a *Final Jeopardy!* clue. Hopefully, not in the category of Notorious.

BRENDAN SHEA recently graduated from the University of Illinois with a PhD in Philosophy and is Assistant Professor of Philosophy at Winona State University. He works on the philosophy of science, logic and inductive reasoning, and the history of philosophy. As a *Jeopardy!* contestant, he would try to avoid State Capitals (unless it's just the Midwestern ones, in which case he might be okay) and Opera.

ELLEN SORG is a lover of *Jeopardy!* who never (or rarely) misses an episode, and she adores Ken Jennings. She spends her days as the Chair of a large English Department in northwest Ohio. Ellen received her Master of Arts in Literary and Textual Studies, and she is kept busy with her ongoing writing and research projects.

DANIEL WANLESS is currently pursuing his PhD in Philosophy at the State University of New York at Albany. He has worked as a Lecturer in Philosophy at Dominican College and as an Adjunct Professor at Berkeley College. He has also spent time as a Visiting Scholar at the Hong Kierkegaard Library at St. Olaf College. In real life he answers in the form of a question and questions in the form of an answer.

SHAUN P. YOUNG is the Social Sciences and Humanities Research Manager for the Faculty of Arts and Science at the University of Toronto. He has a doctorate in political science and has taught at the University of Toronto Scarborough, Carleton University, York University, Brock University, and the University of Ontario Institute of Technology. His research interests focus on issues of justice in multicultural societies, and he is the author or editor of four books and fourteen essays in peer-reviewed journals. Given their similar backgrounds (Canadian, studied philosophy at university, born in Ontario, . . .), Shaun continues to search for the six degrees of separation between him and Alex Trebek.

Here Are the Questions

Popular Culture

1: Who is Alex Trebek?
2. Who is Doctor Who?
3. What is *The Rolling Stones*?
4. What is *The Walking Dead*?
5. Who is Brad Butter?
6. What is *The Simpsons* and Homer?
7. What is *Downton Abbey*
8. Who is Joss Whedon?
9. What is *Psych*?
10. Who is Lady Gaga?
11. Who is Chuck Klosterman?
12. Who is Bob Marley?
13. What is *Dexter*?
14. What is Wilco?
15. What is *Breaking Bad*?
16. Who is Charles Van Doren?
17. Who is Ralph Fiennes?
18. What is Led Zeppelin?
19. What is *American Gods*?
20. What is *How I Met Your Mother*?
21. Who is Johnny Cash?
22. What is the Tea Party?
23. What is *Seinfeld and Philosophy: A Book about Everything and Nothing*?
24. Who is Stephen King?
25. What is *A Hard Day's Night*?
26. What is *The Catcher in the Rye*?
27. Who is Larry David?
28. What is Sherlock Holmes's address?
29. Who is Philip K. Dick?
30. What is *Jeopardy! and Philosophy: What Is Knowledge in the Form of a Question?*?

Slogans

1. Who is Jean-Jacques Rousseau?
2. Who are Karl Marx and Friedrich Engels?
3. Who is Friedrich Nietzsche?
4. Who is Timothy Leary?
5. Who is Lord Acton?
6. Who is Andrea Dworkin?
7. Who is Henry David Thoreau?
8. What is existentialism?
9. What is "Less is More"?
10. Who is Marshall McLuhan?
11. What is "Back to Kant"?
12. What is IngSoc?
13. What is "A diamond is forever"?
14. What is "A mind is a terrible thing to waste"?
15. What is "Politics"?
16. Who is William Henry Harrison?
17. What is "Yes we can"?
18. What is "Just do it!"?
19. Who is Harry S. Truman?
20. What is "Ma, Ma, where's my Pa"?
21. What is "Good to the last drop"?
22. Who is John Stuart Mill?
23. Who is Niccolo Machiavelli?
24. Who is Thomas Hobbes?
25. What is "Better Living through Chemistry"?
26. What is "Knowledge is power"?
27. What is *Animal Farm*?
28. Who is Adam Smith?
29. Who is Jeremy Bentham?
30. Who is Gottfried Wilhelm Leibniz?

Twentieth Century

1. What is bullshit?
2. What is the Chinese Room Argument?
3. What is the Veil of Ignorance?
4. What is "Anything Goes"?
5. What is a fireplace poker?
6. Who is Rudolf Carnap?
7. What is Dice?
8. What is Schrödinger's Cat?
9. Who is Bertrand Russell?
10. Who is Peter Singer?
11. Who is Jean-Paul Sartre?
12. Who is Ayn Rand?
13. What is phenomenology?
14. What is *The Rite of Spring*?
15. Who is Albert Camus?
16. Who is Robert Nozick?
17. What is *Language, Truth, and Logic*?
18. Who is Karl Popper?
19. What is Dialectical Materialism?
20. What is Thomism?
21. What is pragmatism?
22. Who is John Dewey?
23. What was Sigmund Freud's address in Vienna?
24. What is *The Scream*?
25. Who is George Orwell?
26. Who is Whittaker Chambers?
27. Who is Carl Gustav Hempel?
28. What is the numerical value of *e*?
29. Who is Hannah Arendt?
30. Who is Thomas Kuhn?

Potpourri

1. Who is Friedrich Nietzsche?
2. What is the Liar's Paradox?
3. Who is Bernard Mandeville?
4. Who is Maimonides?
5. Who is Thales?
6. Who is Thomas Aquinas?
7. Who is David Hume?
8. What is Ockham's Razor?
9. Who is Thomas Bayes?
10. What is *A Treatise of Human Nature*?
11. Who is Hypatia of Alexandria?
12. What is Helvetica?
13. Who is Jeremy Bentham?
14. Who is Alexis de Tocqueville?
15. Who is Henry David Thoreau?
16. What is the Allegory of the Cave?
17. What are Hypotheses?
18. Who is William of Ockham?
19. What is the unexamined life?
20. Who is God?
21. What is a Turtle?
22. Who is Jean-Jacques Rousseau?
23. What is "To be or not to be perceived?"
24. What is the speed of light?
25. What is Buridan's Ass?
26. Who is Anaximander?
27. Who is René Descartes?
28. What is *The Confessions* by St. Augustine?
29. Who is Heraclitus?
30. Who is the Oracle at Delphi?

Watson's Words

DOCTOR WHO

POLICE BOX

POLICE PUBLIC CALL BOX

POLICE TELEPHONE
FREE
FOR USE OF
PUBLIC
ADVICE AND ASSISTANCE
OBTAINABLE IMMEDIATELY
OFFICERS AND CARS
RESPOND TO
URGENT CALLS
PULL TO OPEN

AND PHILOSOPHY
BIGGER ON THE INSIDE

EDITED BY COURTLAND LEWIS AND PAULA SMITHKA